I0423214

Traveling Light

IN TIMES OF

DARKNESS

One Woman's Journey Through Depression

by

DELL BELEW, PH.D

PUBLISHED BY

GenesisOneDesigns

Acknowledgments

My first acknowledgement and gratitude is to the Lord without whose Light I would still be in Darkness. My second is to my daughter, Jessica, who stood with me through it all. I am sorry that those were trying times for you. If I could have kept it from happening, I certainly would have—and I did try.

I extend my sincere gratitude to the many friends who held the phone, my hand, and my heart as I made the journey. Your love meant more to me than you know, and I know that the Lord has blessed you for being there for me.

Thank you, Don, for allowing me to use your beautiful photo of Tybee Beach, Savannah, GA, our home.

To Bob for making this book a reality.

Table of Contents

Chapter 1: "Traveling Light in Times of Darkness"   7

The "blahs" is a description my mother used to apply when she was having a bad day. What she usually meant was that she just could not get the motivation or the energy to jumpstart her day.

Chapter 2: "My Journey"   13

My eyelids popped wide open as if they were window shades released to fly to the top of the window to expose the daylight; . . .

Chapter 3: "Tears, Sacred Tears"   25

One of the most natural impulses to sadness, pain, or gladness is tears. Tears have many uses, . . .

Chapter 4: "The Light Source"   29

While many things I share here can be achieved by just changing your mind, the real healing and lifetime impact will. . .

Chapter 5: "Traveling Light in the Word"   33

"In the beginning was the Word," and in the end is the Word. . .

Chapter 6: "Talk, Talk, Talk"   43

One of the activities in which I engaged was talking. . .

Chapter 7: "Walk, Walk, Walk"   53

The physical benefits of exercise are well known, but when a person has felt the energy . . .

Chapter 8: "Traveling in Love"   59

Jesus tells us that the first and great commandment is to . . .

Chapter 9: "Mental Diversions"   69

The keystones to traveling Light out of the Darkness. . . .

Chapter 10: "Meaningful Activity"   79

Although a diversion can be meaningful, it may only be a time-filler until bedtime. . . .

Chapter 11: "Sacred Healing Art"   85

One of the most regrettable things I did . . .

Chapter 12: "The Music of Our Spheres"   97

The power of music is undeniable, whether for good or evil. . . .

Chapter 13: "The Dark Side of Darkness"   103

I have stressed the fact that the only way out of Darkness is the Light of Jesus Christ, but . . .

Chapter 14: "Psychotherapy, Counseling, and Medication"   111

I do not presume to give medical advice of any kind, . . .

Chapter 15: "Prayer and Sovereignty"   117

The absolute most important aspect of walking out . . .

Chapter 16: "Traveling Connections"   121

I have saved this information for the last, . . .

Afterword: "There is LIFE out there."   133

CHAPTER 1

Traveling Light in Times of Darkness

The "blahs" is a description my mother used to apply when she was having a bad day. What she usually meant was that she just could not get the motivation or the energy to jumpstart her day. As an adult, I have realized exactly how the "blahs" and "blue Mondays" work on the human emotions. The actual term for these emotions is depression. Depression ranges in severity from mild sadness like the "blahs" to thoughts of suicide. Sadly, almost every human being has had some form of depression throughout a lifetime.

Whether the level of depression a person goes through is mild or severe, depression is a solitary darkness. At best, only people who have been through it can empathize. Whether depression is caused by physical changes, medication, stress, death of a loved one, divorce, or any of a thousand reasons, there are similar symptoms and therapies. The therapies range from time lapse, counseling, support groups, personal meditation, art, prayer, medication, and many things in between. Millions of people suffer from severe depression; antidepressants are drugs of choice for many of them.

I offer this small book to those who are experiencing all forms of depression and for those who have loved ones or friends experiencing depression. At the very least, loved ones and friends can learn that telling a depressed person to get over it is cruel because depression is an evil taskmaster and will not let go simply because we want to get over it. It is the hardest work I ever did in my entire life, and mine lasted eighteen months in its most severe expressions. When it did lift, I felt as if I could finally breathe.

Please share this book with everyone who has had even mild depression or with those who are caregivers of those going through depression. My prayer is that it will lessen the time and pain for those who come after me.

Depression is to the human spirit what pain is to the body. If we did not have pain in our body, we would not seek medical help; but it is amazing how most people live with depression in some form every day without seeking help. Pills can help but know this, dear reader; it is only a Band-Aid for the mind but not healing for the soul.

No one is immune to some form of depression on a regular basis, though we do not identify it as such because there is still a stigma attached. For some, depression is a weakness. There is a song with lyrics that expresses our attitude toward seemingly emotional weakness: "I'll do my crying in the rain." The implication is that when I'm in the rain no one will be able to tell the difference between tears and rain. How duped we have been about some very important things—actually to our own peril.

Depression can become commonplace and we learn to live with it without identifying until that day when it becomes more severe and longer lasting. In many cases, the severe depression is related to some radical change in a person's life, such as the death of a loved one, financial ruin, diagnosis of terminal illness, loss of a job or relationship. The more severe cases brought on by negative change are easier to diagnose but much more difficult to treat because the obvious cause attaches a lifetime of other depressing situations with it. Life becomes like a house of cards—the loss being the card on the bottom.

At that point, all of the other unresolved issues seem to fall in on the top. That was my experience with divorce. While divorce brought it to a "head," I found a multitude of things that needed to be treated, things that had been responsible for a lifetime of mildly depressing times. When I write about depression, I do so with MUCH experience in dealing with the cards that fell in on top of me.

When I went through a divorce, I was catapulted into a wide range of symptoms and reactions from continual crying to anxiety/panic attacks. I feel certain what I experienced was about as bad as depression gets without suicide. I would never want to go through those eighteen months of my life again, but I would not trade the freedom and joy that have resulted from that time for any amount of money. What I share in much detail and examples in my book was wrought with pain of the greatest magnitude. It took that magnitude to shake the brokenness loose and make me a whole person.

I will be sharing my moments of revelation in the hopes that readers will relate and be open for the Lord to reveal root causes and Kingdom solutions to whatever level of depression you are experiencing. I obviously cannot share everything in one book, but I identify some things that you can do or share with someone else. I am not a psychologist or psychiatrist, but I know things they do not know unless they have experienced this kind of depression. Book sense isn't the same as real life experience. I liken it to someone who has had a baby trying to explain to a man what being pregnant and in labor feel like. I know the Darkness—there is nothing to compare it to in this life. It is a force to be reckoned with and Jesus has paved the way for that to happen.

If you are settling for mild depression or sadness as a way of life, **stop now** before it becomes the bottom card on your house that can cause the whole thing to topple.

Depression, as emotional pain that leads us to seek help, can be the best thing that ever happened to you or the worst. You can be your best friend or worst enemy. It really is up to you. Making up your mind NOT to be depressed and not to succumb to living a life of darkness and uncertainly is the first step to getting out of the dark place. Be careful if you have lived long with depression in any form as it can be addictive, especially if it becomes a way of life.

What I share is specifically Christian, but the same steps can be adapted to those outside of the Christian faith. However, if you want the most power and the most healing, turn first to the Lord Jesus Christ and commit your life to him; he alone has the depth of revelation to make you whole for a lifetime and beyond.

Let me explain why I titled this book *Traveling Light in Times of Darkness*. I learned after months of pain that I was able to pull myself up out of the dark pit through constantly running to the Word of God, through both written form and the verses that the Lord would bring to my memory. There were a myriad of ways that the Lord spoke to me, even billboards. In all, it was the Light that brought me out and it was in the dark that I learned to see the Light. I wrote a short poem about that experience that sums up my time in the prayer closet:

Resurrection and Redemption

Before I died,
My life wasn't worth living.
Before I loved,
I didn't know resurrection.
In the dark,
I learned to overcome darkness.
In the flames,
I learned to walk in fire.
In life,
I died a thousand deaths.
In love,
I lived forever.
Now that I love,
You shall live also
In me.

The expression "traveling light" is borrowed from one of my former pastors, Joseph Smith. He preached a sermon in which he said, "If you are going to travel far, you'd better travel light." This, of course, has to do with the weight of one's baggage, which can actually be spiritual experiences that manifest themselves as heavy baggage.

The key to walking in the Light is love. Love is a most difficult word to define, so it comes across as pithy when people make that kind of declaration. I'm quite sure my definition might be the same pithy meaning, like what the world needs now is love; however, I walked it out and I know firsthand that it is true.

Praying for my ex-husband during those months helped me direct my attention toward his good rather than the anger that might have consumed me. Unfortunately, and on the contrary, I had turned that anger inward, which I learned from one of my student's papers was the root cause of depression. I share this story later. For me, I learned a lot in the process of waiting, but I cannot say the time was wasted at all.

Timing, however, is everything.

CHAPTER 2

My Journey

My eyelids popped wide open as if they were window shades released to fly to the top of the window to expose the daylight; and my body hummed as if my finger had been forced into a light socket while I slept. For a moment, while dawn's light peeked through the trees outside of the bedroom window, I lay very still under the shroud of disillusionment and disappointment. Four months, twenty-seven minutes, and thirty-two seconds after the first shock, I mourned the fact that I was awake; and waking meant continuing the battle to maintain my sanity one more day. The operative word is "battle."

Each evening, when I could settle my weary body under the "wedding ring" quilt I had ordered from QVC a couple of years before, I was optimistic that I would sleep well—which I usually did unless my imagination was seared by some good "friend" or relative calling with another sighting of the ex and would give a detailed description of his arms wrapped snuggly around his girlfriend's shoulders at The Comedy Club. My imagination turned on me from time to time and painted all-to-real images that tormented me until the night shades fell down again upon my warped reality.

Most evenings, the quilt and the comforter sheltered me from the fatigue of the long days of labor and jangled nerves. Every day that seemed "normal" inspired hope in me that the next would be the last of the stalking enemy. When I had somewhat normal days, I imagined that the next morning I would awake as if from a dream and find that all was really normal again; that is, until I realized I didn't know what normal was, nor did I ever know—and still do not. Somewhere in my subconscious the ethereal thought lingered that I would awake without anxiety, but that thought laid buried deep in the darker corners where the doors remained shut until the timer would go off and light would reveal the frightening path through the maze. "Normal" eluded me morning after morning.

The eye popping and body humming evolved over time. In the beginning, I awoke on a wet pillow and continued my frantic day trying to hold back the dam of tears. When I could leave campus where I taught English, I let the dam loose and cried the twelve miles home, at once relieved to be away from people and wondering how I would survive the afternoon and evening. What would it be that day? What method would I use to just make it through the rest of the day until a decent bedtime?

Life with all its joys and complications has a strange way of spinning a web that sometimes becomes a habitation that is both a safe zone and a trap. Regardless of how life is happening, it behooves us to pay close attention. Mean and despicable creatures hover near and sabotage events without our notice. This happened to me.

Most of my married life was a conglomeration of emotions, as are many people's. I had found ways to cope and survive for many reasons, some more noble than others. By the time we had made it for more than 25 years, I had faced the fact that in the bad times I would grin and bear it, thinking, "*This too shall pass.*" It always did. I had no way of knowing that my husband's coping mechanism was leading him into a danger zone for both of us.

Let me quickly say that this story is not a husband bashing and is not a testimony of blame—for either of us. Life happens, as they say, and it took two of us to make the mess of our lives. It is about the effect of a life-altering experience that dragged me into a place of absolute darkness. My ex will have to tell his own story.

Some causes of depression are peculiar to divorce, but all of the effects can be devastating for a wide range of causes. The healing measures I share here work in Darkness no matter how you got there. The only sure path out is the Light of Christ.

Now, back to my story of traveling in the Light through and out of Darkness, my personification of depression. In the midst of a busy life teaching English at a Christian college, my best-laid plans erupted, and the places I thought I had under control flew out everywhere. I knew my husband was undergoing a change because he became more easily angered, especially at me, but I had no idea why until he approached me with some strange remarks that I interpreted as his asking for divorce.

Initially, I cannot say I was surprised or disappointed; we had resorted to those conversations on a few occasions in the past. We spoke briefly that day of what we wanted in a separation agreement and that was that. Because we had done this before, I "assumed" it would be over in a matter of a short time. I even thought as I lay in bed later that evening, *"This is not the answer. I'll call him tomorrow."* [A word of explanation: he was working out of town and had already left that evening.]

We talked the next day, but to my surprise, he had set his mind to go through with the divorce this time. That was my first shock. The second was the discovery of another party factored into his equation, a woman at work who evidently gave him the guts to take the leap. At that point and to this very day, I cannot comprehend his thinking—nor can he, I suspect.

15

I cannot say strongly enough how the mere shock of the experience hurled me headlong into the pit of Darkness. Perhaps it was the shock, the unexpected realization of an illusion of which I had been possessed for 29 years. These shocks were responsible for one of many causes of depression by events or circumstances; the death of a loved one and divorce just happen to be two of the major ones. It has been said that divorce is like death except we do not bury the bodies.

My life had made a radical change at age 28 when I dedicated my life to Jesus Christ. He had made all the difference in my life with my husband, children, and extended family members. There had been a couple of really good years between my husband and me, so there were aspects during the 29 years that kept me going, kept me moving forward in pursuit of all that I felt was right and pleasing to the Lord. I had been clinging to the Lord during times of joy and sadness; knowing that he was my rock had held me firm when my world shattered in thousands of ways. He gave me the wherewithal to pick up the scattered pieces one by heavy one.

I guess I always wondered how I would react if that ever happened to me—infidelity—but I think I had put up a brave face to him and said, "*I would definitely leave you and take everything you have.*" Things do not look the same when it happens.

My first reactions beyond the shock were tears, many tears, day and night. I had been a proud person who never wanted anyone to see me cry. That all changed immediately. I found that I could not stop crying silent tears at first. I ultimately had to quit wearing foundation makeup because it stayed streaked. I also had to change from tissues to a cloth handkerchief because tissues crumble and leave lint all over everything. Cloth hankies had a soft and soothing touch almost like having Grandma there to help wipe the tears and tell me everything is going to be all right. Another warm fuzzy that occurred during those early experiences was the warmth of my clothes when I took them off, especially in the winter. I had never noticed how my bodily warmth affected my clothes. I would hold them up to my cheek and imagine it was someone else assuring me everything would be all right. In a sense, it was the affirmation that I was still alive. I was neither dead nor living in a nightmare.

In retrospect, I know the tears were soothing in some strange ways; they gave me the feeling of a little girl whose favorite doll had been taken away and that if I cried someone would get me another one. Though the analogy is simple and childlike, the feelings were anything but.

The feelings of abandonment and rejection rushed over me like waves of electricity and caused me to feel desperate and think about ways to get my husband to change his mind. I was fighting to get back my feelings of security and worth. I still maintained enough pride to keep me from doing stupid things or things I might regret. I stood at my kitchen window one day as my ex drove away with our fourteen-year-old daughter for the weekend and thought, or maybe I prayed, *"I hope someday I will be glad to be divorced."* I longed for the feelings of those days when I wanted a divorce, but they did not come for nearly two years—two long years.

My days became filled with determination to get up and go to work. The beginning of the divorce came during the summer when I was not teaching. By the time I had to go to my faculty orientation for fall classes, I was a divorced woman. My colleagues were shocked. I had thought going back to class would be good because my husband had not been connected with my work; my education, in fact, had been brief periods of separation during the week around the middle of our marriage; it had also been a means of escape and coping. There is, of course, much more to the story of my education than a means of escape, but at the time, it

17

certainly gave me a few more years of marriage until we could get through our times of distress.

Sadly, the Darkness followed me back to school that fall. It followed me everywhere. No matter where I was or what I was doing, the essence of Darkness followed me and did not completely subside for nearly two years. There were moments of relief, which I share in my story, but it never completely left until the victory came. It was always present in some form. Perhaps one of the reasons it never left is that I kept my relationship going with my ex and was bringing the Darkness back into my life over and over rather than recovering. I have not known whether that was a good thing or bad for my recovery, but it seemed right at the time to get or keep my family back together in whatever way possible. The sheer act of trying to pull the family back was at least doing "something."

I was determined to try to undo what I felt I had done. Taking the blame for the divorce is another issue that divorced people tend to hang around their necks, but that is not the reason for my Darkness so I will say no more about it except to acknowledge that it happens.

Being on summer break was a two-edged sword when the divorce happened. On the one hand, I was free to take care of matters; on the other, I had too much time on my hands with nothing to do *but* think about how my life was changing dramatically.

During those summer months, I expended a great deal of energy trying to convince my husband that he was making a big mistake. I was careful not to beg or seem needy—too much pride for that. While I thought there was hope, I tried to work through my questions about why this was happening and what I would do if it didn't work. This all kept me busy during the week and he would come home for the weekend as if there was nothing wrong.

Actually, that isn't true. The air was so thick we could cut it with a knife. I tried to act as if, but the threat and suspicions haunted me even more when he was there. It was clear to me that nothing would ever be the same. If I could have cast off the Darkness moving in, I might have realized that change is not all bad.

The human spirit gets twisted up in dire circumstances and cannot think logically. In time it became abundantly clear that no matter how this all turned out, I had to get out of that black hole I was falling into. At some distinct point, I made up my mind that *I had to make up my mind.* This thing, this Darkness was dragging me where I did not want to go. I had to stand up to it and take dominion.

Taking that stand turned out to be the beginning of an 18-month all-out war with multiple battles on a variety of strange battlegrounds, sometimes on foreign fields. Rarely were they the same, so the many coping skills I employed were many. Had I been able to wield one weapon and stop the Darkness each time, I would have been able to walk out. Why it became necessary to prolong the fight, I do not know. All I do know is the Lord was with me every step and every moment teaching and strengthening me. The battle, as I knew, was the Lord's anyway.

There were many ways that I prolonged the war. One was allowing my ex to hang around in hopes that he would come back to his senses and come home to his family. Two years later, I was able to stand up and say, "Enough is enough." I came to the realization that I was worth more than what I was settling for; my life was wasting away. I finally reached the point where I was happy to be divorced—just like I had asked the Lord early on.

Surprisingly, when I said that to my ex, he came back home and told the other woman he could not see her anymore.

Sometimes we hold too tightly to the things and people we need to let go. It took two years for me to gather enough courage to let go. Could it have been that easy? Could I have shortened the time in the Darkness? The answers still elude me and they really don't matter now. Though I would not want to go through that experience ever again, I would not trade the intimate and anointed time with Jesus for any amount of money or even a "prince" of a man.

From this point in my story, I want to explain the nature of Darkness in ways relevant to depression that can be caused by a myriad of events or situations. It seemed to have come in stages with me. It began in sadness, moved to insecurity, then fear, then anxiety and panic attacks, then to more and more Light piercing the Darkness to the point that there was more Light than Darkness. Finally, the Darkness lifted. I felt it literally lift when the last residue departed. None of what I endured in the Darkness released without much very hard work, more work than I have ever done in my life! It was the hardest work I had ever done. It was physically exhausting. I cannot say this enough.

I would not have been able to endure and find the wisdom for the keys to overcoming, minute by minute some days, had it not been for the Holy Spirit's guiding me step by difficult step. The one thing I could not do was stay in bed and pull the sheets over my head as some have suggested they can do. I awoke every morning feeling like my finger had been stuck in an electrical outlet. Staying in bed would mean defeat; the Lord gave me the determination to fight the good fight, first in pure blind faith and then drawing upon what I knew to be true and not what I felt or saw happening in my life.

My feelings told me I was doomed, but my faith told me that I must move forward. I knew if I did not go on to work, I would lose my job and/or my mind. If I lost either, I would lose my daughter and everything I needed to survive. Only one day in two years did I decide to stay home and in bed; I just could not get up. From my bed, I called a friend who is a few years older than I to tell her; her response was, "No, you are not. Get up out of that bed and go to work! Do you want to give your bosses a reason to fire you?" I listened. That is another key in gaining the wisdom to overcome: listen to the voice of the Lord. That day he was speaking through my friend.

Going to work was always difficult because I wasn't eating and felt jittery and weak in the knees when I arose each work day. One day while I was bemoaning the fact that I was too weak to go to work and needed to eat but could not, the Lord spoke very clearly to me, "You are starving your brain. Eat some peanut butter." I am guessing most of you don't think the Lord speaks that way. He did to me that day; I didn't have sense enough to know that not eating could affect my brain.

I spread a thin layer of peanut butter on one slice of bread and carried it with me to eat in the car on the way to school, gagging with every bite. It worked that day to keep me from feeling weak in the knees and became my steady breakfast diet every working day. I still eat peanut butter and cheese crackers on my way to morning classes or anywhere else I have to be early. [I am not a breakfast person—sorry, I know many of you are grimacing right now.]

This is a good place to segway into another very important experience I had with depression. Certain foods, I found, contributed to my feelings of depression, especially the foods that made me feel full or bloated. One key was not to overeat. Feelings of bloating affect the body both physically and emotionally.

The physical part is one we ignore when we are enjoying the food; nutritionists can guide us in choosing the foods that do not have that effect. I believe the foods that have an adverse effect can be different for different people. All I can say is that once I realized that a fairly good day could end with a meal and be the beginning of a miserable night, I started keeping a mental note of which meals brought on the Darkness. My daughter and I ate out a good deal because I could not be in my kitchen, and cooking a meal was out of the question. In fact, doing normal chores was emotionally stressful. For me, those chores were things a wife did, and I was no longer a wife.

One night my daughter was having a friend over and asked me to cook spaghetti and meat sauce. There were more tears in that sauce than tomatoes; no need for salt. With every stir of the pot, the sauce seemed to echo: *"You are not a wife; you are not a cook; you should never have agreed to this; this is too painful."* That pot of sauce taught me how the enemy of my soul badgers with words of helplessness and degradation.

On the other hand, the one element of my depression that ultimately made me feel good was the fact of not being able to eat food. I lost 25 pounds and the physical transformation rang a very positive bell each time I looked in the mirror and pulled out clothes that I had previously outgrown. More than that, I bought some new clothes that were more fashionable and, shall I admit, youthful. At 47 years old, that was a high water mark.

For that reason, I also had some emotional reactions to feeling full at a meal which goes back to my original statement about food. The dread of gaining the weight that had been a source of some depression previously had a threatening effect on the enjoyment of food. These thoughts may seem peculiar to people who have not been in depression nor had a problem with weight and self-esteem, but they are real—more real than this book or Kindle you are holding in your hand.

On one occasion when I returned from a dinner meal, I was feeling heavy with dread. Bedtime could not come soon enough, though I did not usually rush it. I had walked into my bedroom to prepare for bed when the thought occurred to me that I needed a meeting place to sit before the Lord, an altar or a prayer closet. But where would it be? I had an empty bedroom that my son had vacated, but that would not have been intimate enough as it was large and had become my office.

"I know! I'll use [the ex's] walk-in closet! Symbolically, I would be refilling it with the Grace and Glory of God, a place to meet with my new Husband. Next was the question as to what one would put into a prayer closet. I folded up a blanket into a cushion; I walked into the 3' by 4' closet and plopped the blanket down on the floor next to the wall. A peculiar thing took place next; I immediately and instinctively fell on my knees on the blanket pad and fell against the wall, my hands supporting me. I had an immediate vision of people praying at the Wailing Wall in Jerusalem, which came from a painting I had seen the day before. The presence of the Lord who had come to meet me there was powerful in that sacred moment. I had found my secret, sacred space.

I am not sure that I have enough words to convey how that place shielded, fed, comforted, taught, and lifted me out of many times of utter despair, fear, and absolute Darkness. It was not the place, of course, but it was the fact that the Lord was always there before I arrived, ready to comfort and ready to heal. It was an anointed love chamber. I will share some of the more touching moments I experienced there to indicate just what part the Lord wants to play in our times of Darkness.

In Scriptures, the overwhelming word that God wants us to understand is that He wants to be our God and He wants us to be His people. Then He sent his Son to make that possible. Sometimes life gets in the way of that communion and disconnection happens. Disconnection was the most overwhelming feeling I had during my Darkness. The awesome revelation about disconnection comes in a later chapter.

That sense of disconnection worked its way through me for the first 6 months as tears steadily streamed down my cheeks and onto my neck. They literally turned my skin dark brown in their path. Standing before the freshmen writing classes and the literature classes every period, I managed to stumble through because I needed to keep my job. In most cases, the students didn't know what was going on inside; they didn't know how much I wanted to go screaming out of the room. In fact, the first few weeks, I found it difficult to even stay the entire period. Nevertheless, I only missed one day because of my depression, intense emotions, and anxiety.

Although it took me well over a year to understand my condition and know it well enough to be on alert and eventually to sabotage the outright barrage of attacks, I did crawl my way out but only with the Lord's help. Up until then, I could relate to Sisyphus who kept rolling that rock up the hill and watching it fall back down again when victory was in sight. Every time my victory was in sight, it was time to go to bed. Then in the night, the enemy depression would arrest me again and push my rock back down the hill. Almost every day of that first year, the day presented more than one episode and attack of the enemy of my soul that would require endless questions as I cried out to the Lord, "What next?!!"

One of the most probing and angst-ridden questions was "how long will this go on?" I cried out from the most gut-level agony; I sometimes fell in the floor and screamed, "Oh, God, helllllp me!" Paul speaks of groanings that cannot be uttered. That somewhat describes my agony. I must admit that depression was the hardest work I ever did. Let me repeat that depression was the hardest work I ever did. Never let anyone say that a person can just take a walk or a pill. Except for the Lord's being my strength, I do not know where I got the energy and the wherewithal to keep going day after day. But I did keep moving. . . .

I can say that all of those experiences, as painful as they were, taught me a lifetime of lessons on how to be an overcomer. It would not be an exaggeration to say that it almost killed me. I never considered suicide, but many of those days I did not want to live. I was so tired of fighting the battle, but I knew I had to keep moving. . . .

I do not believe for one moment that God was teaching me a lesson so that I could help others, but I learned through all of the tears that I can minister to others going through depression and to lead them out of theirs. In leading others out of darkness, we become shepherds for other wounded sheep. As I write this, I am reminded of a women's conference I attended early in my Christian life. I sat in the meeting, paying close attention to the speaker, when in my mind I heard these words, "If you love me, feed my sheep." I looked around to see if anyone else heard it. This is what I am doing in this work.

What I share in this work are some of the many ways the Lord walked me through the necessary path out of the dungeon I call post-divorce depression: PDD. I pray my experiences will help make your path shorter and your recovery quicker. Move forward out of the Darkness and into his marvelous Light.

CHAPTER 3

Tears, Sacred Tears

One of the most natural impulses to sadness, pain, or gladness is tears. Tears have many uses, such as lubricating the eyes, but their primary function in the Darkness of depression is release. Holding them back ultimately creates pressure beyond the soul's ability to hold them. They are apt to emerge in a variety of unwanted and ugly explosions over which we have no control. Too often they explode on people closest to us at the time. Verbal, emotional, physical, or sexual abuse can be the outcome of pent up tears. Tears are the pressure valves. The psalmist tells us that though weeping may endure for the night, joy comes in the morning (Ps 30.5).

Sudden eruptions and the continual flow of tears usually signal that something is wrong. Women understand this all too well. When hormones shift, we are apt to cry at the proverbial drop of a hat. However, crying became a major outlet for me. Being too proud to let people see me cry previously, I did an about-face during my PDD. The tears began as that steady stream but became gully washers mixed with loud, gut-level screams and deeply felt groans.

"Ohhhhhhhhhhhh, God! Help me!" I would cry on a fairly regular basis, usually accompanied by various positions of prostration from kneeling to lying on my face in the carpet; sometimes I would sit Indian-style and just rock and cry out to God. They were primary examples of what Paul called "groanings" that I could not utter with my own intelligence or my own understanding (Ro 8.26). These kinds of emotional floods went on for a year or more.

To say I was a mess is an understatement, and I would not have wanted anyone but God to see me or hear me. I lost all sense of modesty and pride. As I think of it now, that is exactly the position to which I needed to be reduced in order for God to give the words to my groanings. If you believe that God helps those who help themselves, you have been misled. God helps those who trust in him. There are many instances in scripture where God is moved with compassion toward those who cried out to him in prayer and in tears.

The best example of how God is moved by our tears is Luke's account of the woman who anointed Jesus' feet with her tears and kissed his feet, wiping them with her hair. When Jesus sensed that the woman was being judged, he quickly identified her tears and actions as her doing what Simon had not done. Jesus forgave her for her sins because she humbled herself and honored him (Lu 7).

My individual explosions did not last long each time and eventually became less frequent. On occasion while I was away from home and when the emotions got to be so intense that I needed to cry out, I would get in my car and find the backside of a parking lot to do my emoting. God never failed to show up. Psalm 61.1,2 is one of David's outcries to his God: "Hear my cry, O God, attend unto my prayer. From the ends of the earth, will I cry unto thee. When my heart is overwhelmed, lead me to the rock that is higher than I." In the Darkness, our hearts become overwhelmed and we must cry out to him for deliverance and release. He is our only hope and our very present help.

The spiritual benefit was that God heard my cries and manifested himself in peace, but the emotional and physical benefit was that it allowed me to release the pressure that had built up from trying to "suck it up" and be normal. People expect us to be tough; they are uncomfortable when we aren't because they don't know what to do with us.

For that reason, I kept those moments of deep groaning between God and me.

As time went by and the episodes of extreme fear, panic, and anxiety began to lesson and diminish, I came to realize that the kind of explosions I had was related to another feeling I hate: nausea. At one point in my adult life, I figured out that I could avoid nausea by sticking my finger down my throat rather than lie in bed hoping the feeling would subside. That really helped because whatever was causing the nausea needed to come out. Dear reader, there is a point to this icky example. Sorry.

Crying out to God and/or falling on my face exclaiming, "Ohhhh, God, help me" was like sticking my finger down my emotional throat and forcing the gag reflex to bring the sour or poisonous substance to the surface and out of my spirit and soul. Healing and peace came every time.

In another of David's psalms, we find an awesome example of God's nearness and compassion in our tears:

I am weary with my groaning; all the night make I my bed to swim; I water my couch with my tears. Mine eye is consumed because of grief; it waxeth old because of all mine enemies. Depart from me, all ye workers of iniquity; for the LORD hath heard the voice of my weeping. The LORD hath heard my supplication; the LORD will receive my prayer. (Ps 6.6-9)

I can testify to the weariness of groaning, but I can also testify to the Lord's hearing my cry over and over; no matter how weary I got, he never did. His grace and mercy were new and fresh each time. I never tired of receiving them.

One word of caution at this point; this kind of expulsion in depression can become addictive. Be careful that you see a lessoning of your expressions so as not to become dependent. Just as physical vomiting can remove food to the point that a bulimic patient becomes habitually prone to it, emotional vomiting can become a very bad habit. Our emotions can become like a security blanket or like a friend. Emotional vomiting, therefore, has a limited purpose. God wants to lead us out of Darkness; not make us comfortable there.

CHAPTER 4

The Light Source

"If we walk in the Light as he is in the light, we have

fellowship one with another. . . " (1 John 1.7a).

While many things I share here can be achieved by just changing your mind, the real healing and lifetime impact will come only through a total commitment to Jesus Christ who is the author and finisher of our faith. He is THE Light of the World.

I am a firm believer in the mind-over-matter theories and always have been. Throughout my life I have learned the valuable principles of keeping my life in check by self-examination and willful choices aimed at being and doing the "right" thing. I watch my own actions and other people's actions toward me so as not to be blind-sided. Unfortunately, over the years those habits of mind built up a strong wall that came across as arrogance and pride. I thought I was invincible.

When my life had taken a radical change at age 28, I dedicated my life and my strong will to Jesus Christ. The changes that were both awesome and subtle had gotten my attention. I became an avid Bible reader and became almost consumed by the stories of Jesus in the gospels. Though I did not fully understand the wonderful changes, I was loving my new life. By the time I got to the third chapter of John in my newly acquired passion for the Bible, I realized what had been happening to me. I had been "born again." That was a phrase I had never heard until I found it there. I believe one has to experience it to understand fully what it means.

More importantly, I was falling in love with Jesus as I got to know him. For the next ten years, I had what one teacher, Kenneth Copeland I believe, called a "hand-running honeymoon" with the Lord. Through my changed life and testimony, the Lord also manifested changes in other people's lives. As I entered college in order to go into full-time ministry, the Word that was so firmly planted in my life had to take second and third place next to the phenomenal number of books that were required to complete a degree. That education spanned more than eleven years and 3 degrees. After all, the Lord had called me to get an education; he would understand, wouldn't he?

While I am sure he made allowances, my soul suffered from that distraction and in deeper ways than I had imagined. In that weakened state of my faith, the most devastating experience of my life caught me on the side that had become blinded by a cocky self-assurance and self-defense. Over a 29-year period, with little relief, I had built up defensive walls to counterbalance a marriage relationship that I once deemed as hateful and angst-ridden by both parties. For me, it had been a matter of endurance. Then, almost without warning, it stood right in front of me: divorce. My walls of defense had hidden the signs.

Let me go back to my first thoughts in this chapter. My born-again life with Christ as my savior and abiding Spirit had been otherworldly until I let other pursuits push Him to the side. In my time of utter sadness, I prayed earnestly for reconciliation of my relationship, so Christ assumed the first position once again. It was almost foxhole religion in the beginning. The battle was only on the horizon at that time but Darkness was closing in. I was desperate for answers and deliverance. The enemy and prince of Darkness had shown up, and I ran to the Lord, my strong tower.

All I can say about those first couple of months is that the Lord was my Comforter, but he did not or, perhaps, could not change my husband's mind. It remained tightly closed to any possibility of stopping the divorce. In six weeks from that first mention, we were divorced! Twenty-nine years of marriage ceased with the judge's gavel. It was a dull thud like the slamming of a very large door that temporarily put the lights out in my soul.

In retrospect, I can say with assurance, there was much I had to learn, many hidden issues that needed to be uncovered, and many revelations from God's Word for which I needed to be prepared and opened to receive. Had it not been for the desperate need I had for relief, I would never have been open to those changes and, more importantly, I would not have known freedom. Climbing out of that dark hole became a matter of life and death.

Jesus Christ is our only Deliverer because he is the Light in a dark place. He had been there all along, even when I put him to the side; in fact, he is already where we are going at any given time. One former student going through depression expressed her situation as having fallen in a hole, a dark hole, and she could not climb out. Without the Light of Christ, we cannot see our way out of those holes. In fact, we may not even know we have entered in until the Darkness obscures the path.

Yes, the principles I share here would work for anyone determined to live a sane life in an insane world. The problem is that one would be cheating oneself of a life empowered by God and a future ordained by him here and in Eternity. The benefits are unlimited.

In the long and short run, I had nothing to lose and everything to gain. This notion is an afterthought because at the time, I only knew one way to survive—that was Christ. He promised he would never leave me nor forsake me. I knew too much to do anything else or to call upon anyone but Him.

Let me end this chapter by stressing that I got to a point where I did not want to live—it was too hard, too exhausting—but I never even thought about suicide. I knew that was not the answer. My life became a daily, even moment-by-moment, struggle to save my sanity.

CHAPTER 5

Traveling Light in the Word

"In the beginning was the Word," and in the end is the Word. Everything in between is all about him—the Word, the Logos of God. If we are to survive this life, we must trust that he will be the alpha and omega for us and in us.

My purpose in this work is not to convince readers to believe the Bible is true, but to testify to its powerful and living presence in our lives. Jesus Christ is the Word, not only the Incarnate God, but he is the ever present Almighty power of the living God. He abides with us and in us to teach us and guide us in the Darkness until we can walk in the Light. No other god or transcendent being of other religions can or will do for mankind what the Father and his Son have done or is doing.

Like he appeared to Peter on the water and responded to the three-word cry for help, "Lord, save me," he is ready, willing, and able to reach out a hand and lead us because he is the Light, the very Light of our life's path (Matthew 14). When the storms of our lives are raging, Jesus is there whether we call upon him or not; but he is always ready to reach out his hand and walk us back to safety.

When I speak of traveling light, I refer not only to the Light [Jesus] but traveling "light weight." Jesus says to us, "Take my yoke upon you and learn of me; for I am meek and lowly in heart: and ye shall find rest unto your souls. For my yoke is easy, and my burden is light" (Matt 11.29-30). I knew these words as I had memorized them in my first years of my new, born-again life. My dad told about how the farmers used to yoke a strong animal with a weak one to balance the load and get the most work out of the two. This principle works when we are yoked to Jesus; we use his strength.

In those early years, I had a thirst to know Jesus Christ. As I had passionately read the stories of Jesus' earthly life, I was falling in love with him. Many years ago, Phil Collins penned the words of the popular song based on words on his sister's tombstone: "To Know Him is to Love Him." That could have been in the Bible because the only way to love Christ is to know him. In fact, in 1 John 4, we learn that he/she who does not love, cannot know God because he is love. Simply reading the events and teachings of his life would not make a difference if not for the author himself being there to reveal the significance of the events. The Bible is alive and constantly working in our lives, yet God never changes. We can depend on his yoke to be strong and constant.

The abiding and powerful Holy Spirit makes the words come alive. When we pick up the Bible and our eyes fall upon a verse that has an immediate impact, we think, "I've never seen that before but that was just what I needed." Those are moments of revelation, moments when the Holy Spirit is speaking words of wisdom and knowledge for a specific time and circumstance. We refer to those as a word in "due season."

The Word is alive and immediate. Though we are sometimes foolhardy to open the bible at random, close our eyes, and place a finger on a verse to get guidance, like consulting a horoscope, it is always wise to make yourself available to hear the words in "due season." Those words are empowered and anointed for that moment in time to comfort, enlighten, direct, or protect.

One profound example of this promise happened a few years ago after I had won a bid online for airfare to Egypt. I had believed for a long time there was something in Egypt I needed to discover. One day I made it my business to follow through. Immediately after I gave my credit card information, an uneasy feeling stirred up in the pit of my stomach. I had committed to pay for the trip, so I had to go. Didn't I?

The next morning I was still uneasy, so I sat down with my Bible in hand. I prayed and asked the Lord to guide me about what to do. As I thumbed backwards through the Old Testament looking for "Egypt," my eyes fell upon several instances in Jeremiah. Without scanning the page, I looked down and saw these words, "Do not go down to Egypt for if you do you shall die."

The message was pretty clear! I looked over to the other side and my eyes stopped upon a verse that said, "Again, I say unto you. Do not go down to Egypt for you shall die. . . ." The Word says that by the mouth of two or three witnesses is every word established! I did not need another word. I arose from the sofa and called the travel agency that had sold the ticket. I had scheduled to fly out in a few days. The woman on the other end listened as I explained that I could not go and maybe they could sell the ticket to the person bidding with me who wanted two but got only one because of me. While I was prepared to lose the amount of the fare, she said, "No problem. Your card has not been charged yet so I will cancel it."

Having been unemployed for some time at that point, I was especially happy to hear those words. To follow up on how the word was fulfilled, America bombed Bagdad two days later and there was rioting in the streets of Cairo, my destination, against the United States. It was an emotionally charged climate that could easily have ended in my death. I do not look Middle Eastern so my citizenship would have been dangerously obvious.

The Word of God had come alive in due season and saved my life—and my money. There have been many more instances during my depression that gave me strength. In my prayer closet, I had a Bible and writing tools in the floor for the times when a panic attack drove me to that place of safety.

I would run to the Word and cry out—loudly—"Lord, I need a word. Help me." He never let me down or left me stranded. Sometimes there would be a particular scripture, sometime a page number, and sometimes I would begin reading until I found the word for that day, that moment, or that "season."

The feelings of loneliness would overwhelm me and I would shamefully say to the Lord, "I thank you for being my husband, but I need a flesh and blood man." Before labeling me as blasphemous, know that God can handle those confessions. Nevertheless, I went to my closet and began to read in Isaiah—a place where I spent much time. I came to the illumined verse, "I will send men unto you." I chucked a bit and said back to the Lord, "Men?? One will do.

The following Sunday at church in the sanctuary, one of the men left his family and came to sit with me and my daughter. I was relatively new to that church, so that confused me until I realized what he was doing. He was showing me support. He was one of the "men" God was sending me. Several men of that church became my spiritual covering during the two years of my post-divorce depression (PDD). There was never anything inappropriate about their support, but the strength I received from knowing God had spoken the word of encouragement added another ray of Light to my traveling gear.

When the Apostle Paul was traveling to Rome aboard a ship with other prisoners, God spoke a word to him that also became one of the most powerful words he spoke to me during one of my panic or anxiety attacks. God had told Paul in the midst of a raging storm that the ship on which they traveled would sink but not even a single hair would be lost of any the 276 men, neither the crew nor the prisoners.

When the crew started throwing prisoners overboard, Paul said, Wait! God said that no one would be lost and "I believe God and that everything he has said will come to pass" (Acts 27.25b). The crew heeded Paul's words and everyone was saved. That word became my constant confession when the storms in my head started to rage.

I had assurance that God loved me and had purposed to do or allow only what was best for me to get me to where I needed to be. When the thoughts that threatened to drag me down or throw me overboard began to seep in, I would repeat, "Oh, no, you don't. I believe God and that everything he has said will come to pass and this ain't it!"

My life became a constant bombardment of negative thoughts that I had to combat with the sword of the Spirit, which is the Word of God. The Word of God is never more alive than when his children need him. And never is it more obvious than when we are in the Darkness. The Word has power and anointing for the long, difficult days of depression. I do not believe the Lord puts us in the Darkness because there is no Darkness in him nor even the shadow of turning. However, he pierces the Darkness with rays of Light until we can climb out of the holes that we fall into. The Word contains those rays.

When I was a child out playing in my neighborhood, I would hear my daddy's whistling to signal me home. I not only knew his whistle but I also knew it was because Mama had already called repeatedly without response. The whistle meant urgency; it meant, "Come home and come home right now!" God's Word is our urgent call to move. We are never too far into the Darkness that we cannot hear his distinct clarion call.

When we have heard, we grab our sword. A sword is both an offensive and a defensive weapon that we carry with us to wield whenever the need arises. In order to use it, we have to train ourselves. Training involves creating a habit. With the habit comes the swiftness of use when we recognize the enemy approaching.

One significant rule of defense is to know who the enemy is and how he works. No good football team or soldier enters competition without knowing the maneuvers of the opponent. After many stabs and gouges, I knew I had to use offensive tactics also before the attacks. Over time and with prayer for wisdom, the Lord began to show me the early signs of anxiety and those awful blankets of fear before they fell over me. When the thoughts began to creep in, I was poised and ready to draw my sword to hurl the Word at them. One weapon that is easy to deploy and use is the Word of God. I was grateful for all of the verses I had memorized as a new Christian years before, but the amazing effect of those words in due season was that they were not always the ones I had memorized. The Lord would meet me on the path and hand them to me.

The means by which we learn to recognize the Enemy and see the Lord's hand stretched out is first to open our ears and eyes. This is another aspect of putting ourselves in a position to receive. That may mean being either in a special physical location or a spiritual place. Either way, these are our sacred places, the places in which we best hear the Lord and the places in which we are most sensitive.

My sacred physical place was the prayer closet, but when I was away I carried it with me in my soul. I had a few scraps of paper on which I had written words of the due season and a notebook in the closet; on one occasion I wrote on the wall [in pencil, of course]. When I was away from the closet, I had other items that reminded me of the words.

On my steering wheel, I tied a red piece of yarn that the Marilyn Hickey Ministries had sent me in a mailing. The red yarn symbolized the crimson blood of Jesus that assured me the battle for my life was not mine but his. I had also received a piece of cloth upon which Richard Roberts had prayed for my healing. I penned this cloth to my nightgown close to my heart because that was the part of me that needed healing. I even taped a message from a fortune cookie on my stirring wheel as it was a word in due season.

These articles and their significance may not mean anything to another soul, but they were visible reminders from the Word of God to fight off the effects of the battle of the mind. If I let down my guard, I was overwhelmed and recovery took longer and was more painful. The old comedy program *Hee-Haw* had a segment in which a patient would say to the doctor, "Doc, it hurts when I do this." The doctor would reply, "Well, don't do that!" While we all laughed, the line was true and good advice. Not to make light of spiritual warfare, but it seems we need to listen to the pain and avoid it the next time. Habits are created with practice—the good or bad ones.

After a period of time, I also learned what was likely to bring on an anxiety attack. The entire siege of depression and anxiety became a learning experience, certainly one in which I wanted to graduate and not repeat. I did experience a six-month period of depression several years later, but I never forgot the lessons I learned. This particular depression was brought on by blood pressure medication, one in which the doctor was trying out until he found one that worked for me. So, you see, I have experienced other kinds of depression. None of them are a walk in the park; they are all challenging in their own way. Getting through them requires wisdom on many levels, but all of them have a path out when Jesus lights the path.

Over the course of my lengthy PDD, God's Word held me fast and constant any time day or night through memory and through Christian teachers on televised church programs. One preacher whom God used to guide me was Dr. Charles Stanley of First Baptist Atlanta. Sadly, he was going through separation from his wife of many years at the same time I was. Even though he did not give personal or intimate details of his situation, his sermon topics gave evidence that he was fighting off and through Darkness.

I taped the sermons and listened to them repeatedly because they were not only Biblically based but because they were coming from one who had tested and had been tested through the same Darkness and fire I was going through. The same God who held him and guided him through Darkness was guiding me. His testimonies built my faith; I could trust God and believe everything he said would come to pass. (Acts 27.25)

Another televised teacher that I taped was Mike Murdock. His teachings about the Wisdom of the Holy Spirit were practical and easily absorbed. They were what he calls Wisdom Keys that I could carry around on a metaphoric key ring to unlock gates along the path of Darkness. Mike Murdock's gift is in taking the promises of God and rewording them in more modern vernacular. I still hear him on various Christian programs; his messages and stories do not change much because the wisdom of the Holy Spirit is the same no matter what road we travel.

Joyce Meyer was on television in my town also. Her wisdom and down-home teaching style reached another part of my life. The first Christmas after my divorce, I bought a new television with a built in video recorder/player for my bedroom. Each night at bedtime, I watched the programs I had taped that had words of promise and encouragement. That way I always went to sleep feeling "strong in the Lord, and in the power of his might" (Eph 6.10). Getting a good night's sleep is another important aspect of traveling Light in times of Darkness; it is healthy for body and soul.

There is no substitute for setting the "sleep controls" on the brain before going to sleep. Dreams and subconscious thoughts grow out of the day's activities and the subconscious works hard to settle questions and problems relative to the things that have arisen during the day. Controlling thoughts during the day is vital but at night we do not have complete control unless we set the mind up before sleep.

Putting on the helmet of salvation (Eph 6.17) protects the mind as well. All of the things we do are choices; like learning and using scripture, good choices have to become habits. When we allow thoughts to come and linger, they become strongholds. Strongholds are roadblocks or cliffs that keep us from moving out of Darkness. Because they are structured in the dark, we cannot see them, much less the way of escape. Using the Word rightly spoken to pierce the Darkness is the Light unto our paths (Ps 119.105).

CHAPTER 6

Talk, Talk, Talk

One of the activities in which I engaged was talking. I call it "talk therapy." Though I did talk about my feelings to anyone who paused long enough for me to get a word in, my talking took on a much greater purpose than exploding on unsuspecting strangers.

I remember well one salesclerk at a department store. I was returning a mother-of-the-groom dress. I explained that since I had purchased it, I had lost weight and it did not fit any longer. Like most women, she bit the bait and asked how I had lost the weight. Because I always managed to work my divorce into every conversation, I gladly went on with the story but briefly.

"How long have you been divorced? Only a month? That's why it is still so tender. You'll get over it soon."

She was wrong, but she understood my need to talk. It's a human compulsion to think we are the only ones who have gone through our particular situation. Certainly, we gain a new perspective on life when ours changes dramatically no matter what the reason.

A male friend told recently of an experience he had while standing in line at KFC. The woman standing in front of him turned suddenly and without provocation said, "I have just gone through divorce. If I had known how painful it was, I would never have done it." The story made me realize I was not an oddball for needing to talk to someone, anyone.

I am a talker and come from a long line of women and men who love to talk. As an English professor and educator, talking is my business; before that, I was a hairdresser, so talking certainly factored into my business. Over time, I had to learn to say the right things and make significant choices. As a Christian and student of life, I also knew that words have power. What I think and how my body performs depend on the words that come out of my mouth. Likewise what is in my mind and spirit comes out of my mouth: "Out of the abundance of the heart, the mouth speaks" (Matt 12.34). We need to remember that we are also justified and condemned by the words that we speak.

That's being the case, I watch over my words so that my words did not take me further into Darkness but rather brought me out to the Light. We are told in scriptures that "[d]eath and life are in the power of the tongue: they that love it shall eat the fruit thereof" (Pr 18.21). Whatever "fruit" we desire, whether death or life, will come out of our mouths. I had been a good student of the Word and believed it was true, so I practiced "life" words. At the time of my greatest despair, I clung tightly to what I knew about my spoken words.

I can make small talk when I need to, but I shy away from conversations that go on and on about nothing or that have a negative tone. Some people come into the world with an almost predetermined negative mindset. Previous to my depression and out of kindness, I tolerated some people who called on the phone to talk. Being selfish with my time, I resisted the phone when I did not want to be bothered.

In depression, I had to get very humble about my time and others'. I acquired a long list of people I could call. I learned through my own pain how important it is to have people who will listen. If they are sincerely interested, that is a plus, but if they would only hold the phone while I talked, they were providing a valuable ministry to me. I steered clear of those who would encourage anger toward my ex.

The important aspect of this healing stream is not to bother people too much or too regularly. I did remember from my own selfishness that they would start to ignore my calls—at least those who had caller ID. To avoid this form of rejection, I acquired the long list of friends to call and I made sure I didn't call more than once a week. Even then I would begin my conversation inquiring about their situation, which was my earnest attempt to reverse my own dilemma and reach out to minister to others: "[P]ray one for another, [so] that you may be healed" (Jas 5.16b). In my ministry to others, I was being healed.

Unfortunately, I would turn the conversation to my own situation. Even in my need to talk, I knew I had to watch my words because, as I stated before, I knew one key to survival was watching the words that came out of my mouth. The "right" words were vital to my restoration and my way out. The words were the Lights. To spend long periods of conversation with negative talk was counterproductive to say the least.

In my telephone conversations, I might make a statement or two to rid my mind of the negative, but I would shift quickly to what I knew to be true. I believe strongly that what I see or feel is not my reality. Faith, as the writer of Hebrews reminds us, is the evidence of things NOT seen. Likely, therefore, what I can see is working against faith in what I cannot see. This state of mind and reality is Darkness; with Darkness comes a whole host of other negative emotions like fear, worry, doubt, unbelief, anxiety, rejection, and panic.

As I write this, it seems so simple—but it most definitely was not. My emotions lied to me constantly and the spirits against my soul were coming on strong. It was my working hard not to be a burden to anyone, which may have been a sense of pride. I could not have taken any more rejection, real or imagined. Have I mentioned that depression was the hardest work I ever did in my entire life?

My conversations on the phone went something like this, depending on the person on the other end of the line:

"Hey, _____, how are you? Do you have a few minutes to talk? Have you heard whether you got the job? Oh, great! When do you start? That sounds like something you would really enjoy and the hours fit into your children's schedule."

After giving that person the opportunity to respond and being sympathetic, I would shift to my story about jobs before I pulled the person into my own story of the present day. This was usually the reason for my call because I would be feeling the deep despair, isolation, rejection, or panic that prompted me to call. My beginning story got shorter and shorter as I learned to talk through to the positive confession, which is the real talk therapy.

Usually the burst of faith that stopped the negative flow would go something like this, "But I have to remind myself that no matter how things seem, the Lord's plan for my life will not change. I can only change my reaction to what is happening right now. I have to shift my focus to the Truth and set my mind on how temporary this life is. And this too shall pass."

Depending on the friend, she will be either agreeing or disagreeing so that I usually have an opportunity to minister or witness to her. People are watching to see whether your faith is real and will sustain you. Those who were full of faith added to my faith and we would both be edified; we all have needs to be heard from time to time. As an educator, I find that I have to be sensitive to those who need to talk while at the same time limiting them and redirecting them when the focus becomes negative or disruptive. I do no less with myself.

Never, never, never use friends to feed doubt, guilt, or anger. That is bad for them and you; no one is served in a conversation that is negative as it gives the enemy of our soul's ammunition: "Neither give place to the devil" (Eph 4.27). I had to learn not to blame or speak angry words about my ex as I earnestly sought answers to why this had happened to us. Answers were important but not as much as my becoming a whole person, healed, fully recovered, and better than I was before.

One of the oddest and most surprising listeners I encountered was Willie, my friend's lawn man. I had stopped by one day after school, which was a frequent practice, because I felt like I needed to talk. Most days Ms. Sallie was home and always had time for me. She was ninety years old at the time, an English teacher, and a Christian.

I was always disappointed when she had company, but that day I was doubly disappointed because I really needed her undivided attention. I almost drove by, but Ms. Sallie saw me. I walked up and joined in their conversation. Willie had finished her lawn and after she introduced me, she went inside to get her checkbook.

By the time Ms. Sallie went into the house, Willie knew why I had stopped by. He turned to me and started speaking words of faith over me. Almost every word that came out of his mouth was scripture. I can't say I had every talked with anyone so fluent in the Bible and so quick to release it. He was well into his comforting and faith-filled words when Ms. Sallie came back and sat down on the front steps and listened attentively.

After some time, she spoke up with a bit of wonder in her voice, "Why, Willie, are you saved?"

"Oh, yes, ma'am," and he broke loose with his testimony about how drugs and alcohol had ruined his life [the part of his life that Ms. Sallie knew him] until one day he sat on an upside down paint bucket in a lean-two shack he constructed out of cardboard boxes. He had lost everyone and everything in his life and hit rock bottom. One day while sitting alone on his paint bucket in his makeshift house, he came to the correct conclusion that that was no way to live and that drugs and alcohol were not satisfactory substitutes for all that he had lost, the stuff Willie quickly reminded us that the Devil stole from him. Nothing seemed to be getting any better, either. That day, sitting on the bucket, he turned his life over to Christ and the Lord cleaned up his life. He started memorizing scripture to fight off the urges to go back to his old life.

That day he was using them to deliver me from one of the days of Darkness through which I could not see the Light to see my way out. The one thing that was apparent from Willie's words: he had walked in the Darkness, too, and was able to give me the Light. He firmly believed in knowing the Word and confessing it to keep his faith built up. If I chimed in and started quoting one of the verses from my arsenal, he could finish it.

Ms. Sallie and I were both blessed and amazed by the faith that sprang forth from Willie's mouth. We rejoiced at how God had delivered him and filled him with such joy and enthusiasm. I went home that day revived and enlightened. Willie had not simply sympathized with me, he offered Biblical answers. We had revival right there on Ms. Sallie's front lawn--and not quietly!

From time to time after that day, I would give Willie a call, and we would talk for hours—or I should say that Willie would talk for hours. It was hard to stop him once he got on a roll. Most of his words were scripture; each one led to another. I shall never forget one word of advice he gave me about men and women. He said no man likes an unhappy woman. When she is unhappy, he thinks it's his fault. That makes him feel bad. It was good and accurate advice.

One further note about Willie: my grandmother loved the Word of God but she had been dead since I was thirteen years old. Her name was Willie. God knows what we need and knows how to package it.

Like he sent Willie, the Lord sent me many people. Through it all, I learned over and over that words rightly spoken bring healing but speaking THE Word amplifies redemption for the soul. Paul tells the Philippians that they should work out their own salvation, without complaining so that they may shine as "lights" in the world (Phil 2.12-15). We cannot save ourselves in the eternal sense, but because of the Lord's sacrifice, we can be an instrument of saving not only our souls [mind, will, and emotions] but we can bring our souls under submission by "rightly dividing the word of Truth" (2 Tim 2.15) Then we also become "lights" to show the path to others. It is an awesome work all around.

As hard work goes, recovery was sometimes a moment-by-moment crisis that demanded a new coping skill. Every time I thought I was getting better, the Darkness would fall upon me and I would cry out, "Lord, when is this going to be over? When? Can it be now?" My season was not over and there was more to come.

Each occurrence taught me a new skill; each skill was another revelation, another opportunity to test my faith and for the Lord to show forth his might and power in my life. I remember saying on one occasion, "Lord, you must have an awesome work for me to do if I need this kind of faith!" On the occasion of my mother's death, which was in the midst of my Darkness and in the midst of another revelation pertaining to my ex that was a stab in my heart, I knew I had to toughen up to get through what was ahead. I said to the Lord, "You must think I am stronger than I do."

Indeed, he did and I made it through one of the most difficult trials of the Darkness, and just when I did not think it could get any darker.

Through the Darkness, God's Light showed through and led me to the other side of the cave I had traversed as I buried my mother. I stood at her casket and said, "Mama, I don't think you can hear me, but please speak to the Lord on my behalf. I need help." She went to be with the Lord about a year after my divorce and that proved to be another stepping stone in the path out of Darkness. As they say, it is always darkest just before the dawn. I had one more advocate before the throne on my behalf.

CHAPTER 7

Walk, Walk, Walk

The physical benefits of exercise are well known, but when a person has felt the energy that is stored up and threatens to explode, she learns the real benefit, which is to her spiritual, emotional, and mental health.

One of the biggest threats to sanity is anxiety attacks. Walking is just the best means of working out anxiety. There were times during my depression when it stepped up several notches. These bouts were spirits of fear that dropped on me from left field and usually without any obvious reasons.

When fear dropped in, I had to hit the road, which is the road in front of my house. I walked as fast as I could like the fear was chasing me. In many ways, it was. The brisk walk had certain physical benefits beyond expending energy. Walking stirs up endorphins, the feel-good hormones. In a short amount of time, the good feelings would begin to replace the fear. Add to the endorphins the burning of calories and firming up of muscles and you have a recipe for good mental and physical health. Walking also diminishes your appetite, if that isn't already an issue.

These aspects or benefits I learned contributed two things in my walk out of Darkness. First, the temporary benefit of feeling good instead of wretched and fearful made this practice well worth the effort and worthy of adding it to my arsenal against fear and anxiety. The second was physical at first but contributed to my losing weight—25 pounds in all. I not only felt better about the way I looked but also my self-esteem was undergoing a healing. Because the spirit of rejection is such a cruel task master, improving my appearance gave me a hatchet to sling at some of the elements that caused me to fall headlong into that black hole.

At this point, I need to reiterate that although my depression was prompted by divorce, depression is a foe that can be attacked and overcome by some, if not all, of the coping and recovery skills I learned. The reason: depression is an attack on our souls, but the battle has already been won by the Lord of our lives. We just have to endure. The biggest problem with enduring is that we must first decide to do it and then listen to the Lord as to how to stay in the battle until it is over without shadow boxing and eventually succumbing to the enemy. The only way we can fight in the Darkness is to keep our eyes peeled for the rays of Light. Then and only then can we see the path and walk on out.

Now as we are discovering the path to walk out, we participate in building the skills of endurance. Walking, as I have stated before, expends energy when fear and anxiety rev up our hearts and nervous systems. However, there is another major component to the physical and emotional. It is the spiritual.

Almost from the first step out of my door, I began to call upon the Lord, to thank him, and to profess what I know about the Scriptures. Most of the time, I did not have a planned prayer or confession because my head was full of fear, so my first words were simple, "Thank you, Lord." After saying that many times and clearing my head of chaos, another word would come. Often I would shift to particular things I had to be thankful for, like "I thank you, Lord that you are working all things in my life for my good; I thank you that your thoughts toward me are good and not evil. I thank you that your Word is true, and I can believe that whatever you said in it will come to pass." I was calling forth verses from the Scriptures.

There are many such professions of my faith that I literally pounded into my spirit and soul as I walked. My usual path was less than one mile, but in that distance my heart was being restored; afterwards I could go back home to complete necessary tasks for the day. I list some of the great and precious visions and images the Lord gave me during those encounters in a later chapter.

Weather permitting, I walked at least once a day but more if the need arose. I carried walking shoes in my car when visiting so I could hit the road when I felt overwhelmed. Even when I was on campus and had an anxiety attack, I went to the track and the gym. The track was not shaded, of course, and was a hot path but it served a necessary purpose. I had an audio tape that always spoke to my spirit. I'm sure that I listened to it about 300 times by the end of my dark path. The teaching on the tape was about loving the unlovable, but it was about so much more. It gave me insight into my relationship with my former husband. I had to rethink him, so the reason for my Darkness also became a means of recovery. I had several other cassette tapes, but that one was the one I listened to most often.

One of the more physical and aesthetic benefits in walking is being in nature. I lived in a wooded area, so my walk was mostly shaded and beautiful. I always loved trees before, but during those dark days, I became intimately involved with them. My friends call me a "tree hugger." I do not worship nature by any means, but I highly recommend being in nature as much as possible during periods of depression, even the mildest forms of depression. Interacting with nature is the major advantage over walking on a treadmill.

There were also places on my walking path where I was exposed to sunlight that could penetrate my eyes and deliver serotonin, another feel good chemical in the brain, and the necessary vitamin D. Vitamin D deficiency has been linked to chronic illnesses; to increase Vitamin D, you can take supplements, but getting sunlight is by far the best because it solves several problems. I believe the recommended daily dose of sunlight is from 10 to 15 minutes, while not so much as to cause skin damage. Both serotonin and endorphins are brain chemicals that release neurotransmitters to contribute to the feeling of well-being and stress relief; they are by products of exercise especially outdoors. Deep breathing outdoors during exercise has the added benefit of increased oxygen to the brain that also helps the brain function and gives a sense of wellbeing.

Spirit, soul, and body benefit immeasurably from walking, especially briskly. Strolling can help but not to the extent of a brisk walk. At the time of our divorce, we had a swimming pool in which I exercised regularly, so I was already somewhat active. However, the stamina for walking briskly took some time to develop, but the fear and anxiety forced me to do the work. It began with one step out the front door as I traveled out of Darkness and into His marvelous Light.

For those who haven't been active, it may take some time to get accustomed to the rigor. For those who cannot walk, find other ways to move some parts of your body to get the body moving and stir up those neurotransmitters.

DISCLAIMER: This chapter is not intended to be a wellness program in the professional sense, just things I learned that worked during periods of Darkness. You can read more about these brain chemicals and their benefits online. A good place to start is Web MD. I recommend that you consult your doctor before beginning an exercise program, especially if you have health problems other than depression.

CHAPTER 8

Traveling in Love

Jesus tells us that the first and great commandment is to love the Lord our God with all of our heart, soul, and mind (Matt 22.37, 36). The reason is that God is love. He does not merely have love or give love, he is love. To love is to be directly, immediately, and intimately intertwined with the Spirit of Love. To do otherwise is to walk outside of his divine love and protection.

Paul said in the "love chapter," 1 Corinthians 13, that if we have prophecy, understanding of mysteries, all knowledge, and all faith but have not love, we are "nothing." Nothing that we have and nothing that we become are profitable to us or to anyone else. Love is not only the greatest commandment, it is the essence upon which all of life spins and has its being, which includes us.

Like anything that we cannot see or touch, love takes on a very subjective reality, almost to the point of obscurity. I am amused when people use phrases like we should "love" one another or we need to just get along as if that were an easy thing to do. When the rubber meets the road and we find ourselves having to put our love for God or for one another to the test, we come up short or lacking in the ability to do that.

The person that was hurting me the most in my time of Darkness was my ex-husband. I should have been loving him all the time, but finding love for him in pain was an insurmountable problem. Yet I had to do it, and I knew that very well. It was not an option. But how would I do that?

* * * * * * * *

When I was 19 years old, I was dating a young man who actually acted as if he just couldn't live without me and that I was the best thing since sliced bread. [By the way, what's so good about sliced bread?] I digress. He was what girls called today "needy." Nevertheless, one day it occurred to me that he was dependable and that I might do well to return his emotions. I made a **decision** to love him. I did and we had a very close relationship; life was good and I felt that the world was a brighter place.

Then I married him. The love wavered dim under the weight of his smothering and controlling expression of love. Something must be seriously wrong with the picture that I had painted in my mind of what our love should be. When I told my mother at the two-week mark of our marriage that things were not going well, she let out an "Oh, no, Dell." It was after that conversation that I decided once again to make this "love" work its way through the bad times. I did that for 29 years; it was never smooth and easy. It hurt like hell a lot of the time, --but I had **decided**.

Then the day came that the marriage was over because he fell out of love with me; that is, he decided he didn't have any feelings for me anymore. Sixteen years later it is still a mystery to me how someone can decide not to love someone after all those years. He had become to me like a member of my family that I could no more really divorce than I could divorce my mother or father. I expressed it this way: you cannot unscramble eggs. The love decision I had made mentally and emotionally had grown into the agape, God kind of love.

I think it would have been a lot easier to have hated him or at least to have been angry with him, but I could not unscramble those feelings from reality. I see people get out of one marriage and into another fairly soon, especially men, and I cannot understand how that works. I guess it's because I haven't found another person that I like well enough to **decide** to love.

Now back to how I decided to rectify my feelings at the time of my Darkness and allow the Light to transform both of us. I can only say that these were not my doings, this love solution; like everything else in my Darkness, the Lord was leading me into and through because I could not see the path. I made another decision to love my now ex-husband. It was not as easy a decision as the first time because I had to climb over a lot of hurt and pain and the disturbing questions. It was certainly easier than the alternative, which would have put me at odds with God. Unforgiveness is not an option. I could not afford nor did I have the strength to carry the weight of my own baggage that would not be forgiven in the process of my withholding it from my ex. Forgiveness and love work together.

The tape that I listened to over a hundred times by Malcolm Smith about loving difficult people kept reminding me why and how I could love him. Smith taught me who the real enemy of my soul is and it is not my ex because, in fact, he was victim to the enemy of his soul. There are probably more experiences from this aspect of my walk in the Light out of Darkness than any other but, suffice it to say, God used me as a conduit during those months. No one so miraculously used for such a high calling could have been more blessed or more anointed. Having God's divine love flowing through me strengthened me for the journey to be sure.

Deciding to love my ex was a tall order because for most of the 29 years we were married, he had inflicted emotional and verbal pain on my spirit. He had beaten me down so low on a number of levels—though not physical—that somewhere along the way, I had had to decide that if I was going to be who I was called to be, I would have to do it on the side. I would fulfill all of my duties as a wife while pursuing the plan God had for me. I did not shirk my duties but neither did I give of myself in any spiritual way to him. I can't answer the questions about how God figured into that part of my life, but I do know my emotions were superficial and mechanical. I just did not know how to do anything else.

Then the tearing of flesh in divorce severed all of that superficiality and left me in a heap on the floor of the ex's closet, now my sacred space. The range of emotions at first was vast, but I soon came to the realization that I had to forgive him. To do otherwise, as I've said, is not an option. The last thing I needed was for God to withhold his forgiveness toward me.

The need to love and bless my ex came to my remembrance when I drove to Atlanta to a church that was known for its deliverance ministry. I had become tormented at one point by my ex and his "girlfriend." Everywhere I went in public, I was afraid I would see them together. There were times when I thought I did see her in department stores, even out of town. I looked at cars in restaurant parking lots to make sure they were not there. I felt the paranoia seizing control of my life so I sought help.

The trip took about four hours. I arrived early to the church and went in for information about when the service began and so forth. The pastor was already there so we talked briefly in the hallway. I explained my torment.

Without hesitation, he told me I did not need deliverance, which was good news. I just needed to pray for the ex and girlfriend every time they came to my mind. The devil was bringing them to mind to torment me, but the last thing the devil wanted was for me to bless them. If I did that each time the thoughts came, the thoughts would quit coming—and so they did almost immediately. The pastor had not only told me what to do but told me why it would work. It was a long-lasting, far-reaching "cure."

That had been my decision to act in love and I learned the truth of the scripture, "Perfect love casts out fear" (1 John 4.18). I include the story about deciding to love just as I had decided to love my ex before he was my husband because I had to keep on deciding when he was not. As I saw him suffering and struggling through the divorce, I had empathy for him although I could not understand why he was putting us through the Darkness. I still do not.

Many people come through our lives and bring with them a myriad of emotions and experiences. We can't always prevent them from doing emotional damage, but we can decide how we will respond and whether we will let their effects stick to us. This is never truer than in divorce. How we walk through the pain or relief is a decision.

One case in point: My sister was going through divorce a few months before I did. Our post-divorce experience was totally different. The reason: we were all four different personalities and our couple dynamics were different. On the surface, my sister and I should have been able to lean on one another, but we did not. Our highs and lows happened at different times. When she was on a level field, she had no patience with me, and when she was on an emotional low, she didn't want my help. What our experience showed me is that the way we react or handle depression can be very individual experiences.

However, there are common experiences and the Lord remains the same and so do his spiritual laws. What worked for me will work for anyone though I realize not everyone will seek the Lord. Loving a person who hurts us or who means harm, even in a work situation, is a key to disarming them and their influence, especially if fear is attached because, once again, perfect love is the difference. Being willing to love or do good to those who despitefully use us turns on the Light that causes the Darkness to flee.

In those places we learn that love is not a feeling; he is a person. When we decide to love, we bring him on the scene. On one of my brisk walks, I had been praying and confessing the things for which I was thankful; I had a vision of a cocoon. With that came a spontaneous prayer for the Lord to build a cocoon of protection around my ex. While he was in the cocoon, I asked the Lord, the Holy Spirit, to love and minister to him. That became a regular prayer. My ex was swimming in some treacherous waters and I knew he needed protection. The prayer also gave me patience because I knew that answers would come in the Divine right time.

Sometime later, a minister told about what happens to butterflies when humans try to help them out of their cocoon before their time. The process of fighting to get the cocoon off strengthens the wings of the butterfly. If it does not reach its potential, the wings will not work and the butterfly will fall to the ground and die. We are exactly the same; when our path is interrupted and we have not achieved all that we should before moving on, we wither and sometimes even die.

* * * * * * * *

In a chapter about love, one expects to find the essence of God's love and his commandment that we should love one another. Jesus said that we should love one another as he has loved us (John 15.12), which is a very tall order.

But another, perhaps more difficult, need we have is to love ourselves. As I walked through PDD, the most agonizing emotion was rejection. The very nature of rejection suggested there was something so inherently wrong with me that my husband felt that he could not only abandon me but could choose someone instead of me. The spirit of rejection wounded me in so many ways that I developed self-loathing, which was one of the last revelations the Lord gave me upon walking out of Darkness.

He withheld that one until I was ready to not only know but to be healed. The revelation came the day before I left for England for a conference. As he spoke those words to me, I had replied, "Oh, God, I don't want to hate myself. Teach me how to love myself."

Within 24 hours those lessons began. The World Congress of Poets involved participants from 35 countries and most of them, as it turned out, were Christians. Over the course of the week, I found many new friends who at least seemed to appreciate me and what I contributed to the Congress. One day, in fact, I read the poem included in this book in which I expressed the frustration of not being heard, "No One's Listening."

As I returned to my seat, a couple of Japanese women behind me tapped me and said in unison, "We're listening." They had no idea what their comment had meant to me. Several others in the group bonded with me that week and we forged a firm relationship. I even moved to Pennsylvania where they lived, believing as I did that that was what God was directing me to do, which is a story for another book. It was a major leap of faith and a culture shock for many reasons.

Had I not been fortified by my new love for myself, I would never have entertained such a crazy idea. I had prayed and waited on God to confirm the move for seven months. Without fear, I packed all of my belongings and my daughter and headed north— 850 miles to be exact; perfect love had cast out fear.

Before I moved to Pennsylvania, I took an appointment as pastor of three United Methodist Churches in the rural area near Punxsutawney. That first year was not an easy one, but the lessons I had learned and the faith in the Lord's being with me, I stood firm while at the same time moving forward. One other connection to Pennsylvania was that the man with serious heart trouble was in England and lived in Pennsylvania. [That story appears in another chapter.] I only learned that the last night we were in England at the World Congress of Poets. The Lord had taken him to Georgia to lecture where I was teaching at the time. He was my connection to England, although I was one connection to God's plan for his life. I discovered from learning his story that he was a walking time bomb.

I stayed in Pennsylvania for five years before the Lord lifted the anointing to be there. That prophetic word took me and held me there until it was time for me to move on. When it was time, I physically felt the release. I took a teaching position in another Pennsylvania town for a year before getting back south—home. And here I sit.

I share this part of my life story in order to confirm that there is life after the Darkness. My life in Pennsylvania was extraordinary in so many ways; there were experiences that I would never have had except for my divorce and subsequent PDD, though I do not recommend divorce as a travel agent. Mine was a very big circle with some larger-than-life changes, and many great accomplishments—the half has not been told and I will not know the impact of my painful journey through Darkness until I am walking in the full Light of God in Eternity.

CHAPTER 9

Mental Diversion

Previously I have suggested that keeping the mind under control and retraining it are keystones to traveling Light out of the Darkness. Another aspect of taking control is diversion. Through diversion, you put your mind on another track. The track is a parallel path out of Darkness, so you are still moving forward, depending of course on the choices you make for diversion.

Being determined to push through the Darkness leads to a search for healing, so the diversion can be an important tool for education. By this I mean, use your diversions to find healing. I discovered after I was already doing this that reading had a two-fold purpose; it took my mind out of the fear and anxiety mode and helped me seek answers to the "why" questions. Whether it produced answers or not really didn't matter as much as the diversion.

Reading was one of my diversions. The time that I realized that reading had healing qualities was on a trip to Atlanta to a literary conference. The trip occurred in the darkest period. Driving the four hours to Atlanta and being in that chaotic city were the last things I wanted to do, but I had to go. I had worked up through a couple of responsibilities in my particular session, the Conference on Christianity and Literature, to become the chair that year. As the chair I had to choose the papers that would be presented at the conference and I would be introducing the speakers. Professionally, this trip was significant.

The fear of driving that far from home with my daughter, who had not learned to drive, was paralyzing. My aunt, who was also a college professor, had agreed to meet me there and spend the weekend. Because she had already been a source of comfort and guidance, her being at the end gave me a boost. I learned as I was already packed that she could not attend. Nevertheless, she had given me what I need to move forward.

My daughter and I made the trip safely, checked into the Marriot, and located the meeting place, which thankfully was in the Marriot. I took a Benedryl tablet to calm myself down. By the time I had to lead my session, I was cool as a cucumber. My colleague complemented me on my presentation, so I knew I had made it! I did nearly fall asleep during the reading of the other conference papers, however.

When my session was over, I went to an underground mall where I found a bookstore. The last thing I needed was another book, or so I thought. I found a book entitled *You Can Feel Good Again* by Richard Carlson. I purchased the book and went back to the Marriot lobby to read. Why, you may be asking, did you not go back to the room where it was quiet? That is a good question.

The lobby was a large atrium in which I could see all of the floors and their balconies. I could watch our room where my daughter had gone to watch television. The biggest draw to the lobby was that there were hundreds of people going and coming, so I did not feel isolated or abandoned. As I sat in one of the many overstuffed chairs, I began to read my book.

The book was categorized as "self-help." The premise of it was that we could think our way out of the bad times and into the good. Though the author never gives due credit to the original author of this idea, the idea is "As a man thinks in his heart, so is he" (Pr 23.7). I didn't fault him for that; he gave example after example of people who had changed their lives and circumstances by changing their minds [thinking].

I knew the premise quite well, but the beauty of the book for me was right time, right place. I sat in that lobby for hours reading and thinking, changing my fears, anxieties, and depression into hope and recovery. By the next morning I was ready for the trip home.

I cannot say how depression affects other people, but one of the debilitating aspects for me was occasional disorientation. Though I had previously been an independent woman who had no apprehension about traveling and no problem following maps or internal navigational devices, on this trip I found myself sitting at the opening out of the parking garage not having any sense of which way to go. The fear of going out into the world had me stuck. The fact that it opened into a one-way street helped me decide, but I was coming out on a different side of the building and knew I would be turned around and basically lost.

That feeling among the many others associated with depression was something I could not control when it came. That is, I couldn't keep it from coming, but I was learning how to overcome and keep moving forward. For that weekend, having the book to read had gotten me through another experience. Once I got on the right road out of town, I was able to drive us home.

I began this chapter speaking about diversions. In many cases, books provided the mental diversions and helped me pass time, which had become most necessary. I kept thinking if I kept moving forward, I would eventually move out of the Darkness. With the Lord's help, that was happening moment by moment.

The first rays of Light came through reading the Bible, which I did constantly, so this is my first recommendation for reading for diversion. The second would be anything that teaches or reveals answers, whether it is another's story or some psychological response to the questions you are asking. These can be secular or Christian because God can speak through anything, even billboards.

One book that has been a very close second to the Bible because of its prophetic words is *Come Away My Beloved* by Frances J. Roberts. I have had the book since the late 1970s and it is so dogged-eared that I can hardly keep it together. The cover is long gone and I had to go online to get the exact author's spelling before I could recommend it. There are new copies available, but I refuse to part with my old, beloved copy. The aspect that makes this book so awesome is that it is anointed. Besides the Bible, I have had many, many instances of enlightenment in "due season" from this book. I have indicated dates in the margins when I turned randomly or received a page number in my mind. On some occasions I wrote a note.

I would go months without ever looking at the book when it would suddenly come to mind. Not only were the words appropriate but they also contained certain words that confirmed that they were for due seasons. Those times always cause faith to rise up in me. During my PDD, I went there often but mostly when the Spirit led me there. The book is written in first and second person, as the Lord is speaking directly to the reader. I have read several devotionals and have even written one myself, but none so powerfully anointed.

As I was writing this piece, I decided to go online and get some information about the author. Her obituary reads like I would like for mine to read. She passed away in 2009 at the age of 91. Her book sold over a million copies, although it was one of many. She was a musician and song writer involved in child evangelism. I never felt the need to know this information because the book was so beautifully written, that the hands that penned the words did not matter as much as the source. I give the book on occasion as gifts and I pass this information on to you as my gift.

Another example of a book that had significance in a slightly different way was one that I discovered late one night. That night as I lay in bed reading, the Lord brought to my mind the promise that "all things are possible." As I pondered that positive word, I looked over to my bookshelf near the bed and spotted a book entitled, *All Things are Possible.* Coincidence? No way. That was one of the hundreds of ways the Lord had of letting me know that he was speaking to me. The book is a collection of faithful leaders of the Charismatic renewal and all that they endured as God anointed them to spread the Gospel.

The book not only diverted my attention but it also filled my heart with faith and anticipation of what God was going to do in my life through this miserable Darkness and, in fact, what he was doing already in my life at that very moment. Books about how others endure and conquer obstacles bring the Kingdom to us. I was reminded constantly that I am not a slave to this world and all of its chaos, but I am a significant citizen of the Kingdom of God. The things I can see have no hold on me. The things I feel are liars to shroud a greater purpose.

When we are engulfed in the Darkness of depression and fear, we forget; but the testimonies of others who have travelled toward the Light and emerged victoriously remind us that we, too, will emerge.

There were other secular books that taught me how to think about my situation and answer those why questions. If I gave the titles, you might laugh or be aghast. While I do not believe or accept everything in those books, there were some points that provided keys to what my ex might have been thinking. The thoughts were positive diversions because they kept my mind busy thinking about something logical. As with all that we experience, my thinking about life and relationships was shaped by the bits and pieces from all of the books I read.

The most important aspect of the reading material at the time was that it relieved me momentarily of the mental and emotional stress. I hasten to say emphatically at this point that you need to pray for discernment before you read anything. You can easily be lead astray so that you move from one place of Darkness to another and go further into not only depression but into the bowels of hell.

Books that are fictional can be very helpful as long as you know the Truth projected in the story. All Truth is from God and can heal. God can speak through billboards and through the mouths of sinners if you are watching and listening for his word. If it is Truth that squares with the Word, we can take it to the bank and make a deposit or withdrawal.

One example of the kind of reader I am is my going to see the first *Star Wars.* I was amazed at the correlation between the plot and the Bible story of the war between good and evil, which by the way occurs in many fictional stories and movies. I mentioned this to my husband as we left the theater. He said, "You are the only person I know who sees a spiritual application in everything." Being a literature teacher in addition to a lover of the Bible, I guess I am prone to do this type of interpretation—though I am certainly not the "only" person.

Because I was teaching literature at a Christian private college, I also had to read certain works of literature. I had the academic freedom to choose what my classes read, so I would choose works that were beneficial to both my students and me. Grading composition papers was the worst because the students chose their own topics.

In one research writing class, the students had written their papers on topics that they chose. The papers were longer than usual because they were research projects. This kind of diversion usually doesn't qualify as a positive use of time, but I had to get the job done. I had a responsibility to my students.

When I got down in the stack to a paper titled "Depression," I froze. The temptation was to give the student an A and go on to the next paper. I didn't, of course, so I began to read. About midway through the paper, I read a statement that stopped me in my tracks. It was a giant leap toward recovery and out of Darkness.

The statement: "Depression is anger turned inward." That was it! The answer to why I had fallen into such despair. What had begun as sadness and tears had become despair as I had studied what was happening and what went wrong. No matter where the anger was coming from or at what person it should be directed, the cold hard fact was that I needed to get rid of it. I had pointed the finger at my soul and sent it there. I set my mind to going home and doing business with my Self. I had to forgive myself for whatever I was holding myself hostage.

I went home to my prayer closet and took pen in hand. I made a list of everything that came to mind that I might have against myself or the things I might have done wrong. The list was pretty long and some things might have been ridiculous, but our psyches can sometimes be tough and our psyches can't always tell the difference between what is true or fictitious when it comes to guilt and blame.

Nevertheless, I pointed to each one, read them out loud, and said, "Dell, I forgive you for ___[each thing]___ in Jesus' name. Now, Father, I ask you to forgive me for holding Dell hostage. I call it done. Amen."

The sense of freedom was immediate. I cannot say how long it was after that until total freedom came, but the experience was palpable. The Lord had reached down to my daily tasks and to one I dreaded most and anointed one sentence that worked a miracle. I believe I shared the experience with the student, but she will never know the power of her words in that paper. She may have disliked the task of writing it as much as I had dreaded grading it, but thank God we continued with our tasks.

Circumstances like these were all reminders that while our backs are turned, God is our rearguard. He is never blindsided. Even to this day when I feel the least bit sad or uncertain about how to translate experiences, I can rewind the tape. I can remember that God's love and his provisions are never ending. His will for my life has not changed. God had said thousands of years ago through the pen of a ready writer: "Call upon me and I will answer you and show you great and mighty things you know not of" (Jer 33.3) He is most apt to give us a future with a hope and "turn away [our] captivity" (Jer 29.14).

I learned through my second bout with medically-induced depression that I cannot function without hope—none of us can. When I speak of diversion, I am talking about putting off hopelessness until another time. The means of diversion may not be as much healing as other activities, but it will hold you in check until the healing comes. They are the rays of Light.

CHAPTER 10

Meaningful Activity

A lthough a diversion can be meaningful, it may only be a time-filler until bedtime. Some days that was all 1 prayed for: something to keep me busy until I could close my eyes in sleep. There are other activities that have a purpose that can hold us fast to the path not only out of Darkness but into our Divine calling.

Shortly after my conversion in 1975, I responded to what I believed was a call from the Lord to minister. About the same time, I felt the need to write my testimony. The Lord gloriously saved me and my biological father at the same time; the story is miraculous on several levels as I had never met my father before the day he directed me to my heavenly Father. Although he had gone to church most of his life, he realized later that he needed salvation also. Through a series of circumstances related to meeting me, he, too, received Jesus Christ as his savior. Having a great testimony, I set about to write my story with the intention of publishing it. I got only as far as the typed copy, but now it has a permanent home in my file cabinet, a place no one goes but me.

The need to write led to other "things." As a result of my calling to ministry, I had begun a college degree at age 31 so that I could ultimately attend seminary. After I had finished my bachelor's degree, I had decided to put off seminary: a long story.

Instead, I told myself, I will get a graduate degree in English because I wanted to write. At least if I had a Ph.D. in English, publishers might read what I write before putting it in File 13. That has proved to be false, by the way.

Nevertheless, I continued on to graduate school and ultimately did finish a Ph.D. in English. One thing I never considered was that I would actually learn to write. That turned out to be an eleven-year writing course! Two of my colleagues told me I should write. When I finally got around to seminary, one my professors said he hoped that whatever direction my ministry took it would include writing.

That suited me just fine given my past leanings. The more important aspect of that "calling" was that the Lord was giving me things *to* write. He was unveiling some amazing revelations that compelled me to write them down.

One such revelation held me fast during my darkest periods. The thesis of psychotherapist Viktor Frankl's book, *Man's Search for Meaning*, is that man can survive almost anything if he has a purpose and, therefore, a reason to live. Frankl believed that when a man suffers, he has to find a reason for the pain. He knew this very well as he rewrote a book in the prison camp that the Nazi's had previously taken from him. He had lost his family in the prison camps, so he had no one to go home to, so writing was his purpose and it gave him meaningful activity. If purpose can give a man the will to survive in a Nazi prison camp, it can certainly give us the wherewithal to travel lightly out of our own Darkness.

The passion for writing down my revelation came sporadically. I would write feverishly for weeks and then lose steam for three months. The book that grew out of that revelation took a total of eleven years to finish, long after I walked out of Darkness. The last five years of that was a period of unemployment, which has its own form of depression at times.

Actually, I could say the Lord was employing me because he sheltered me while I wrote.

He had tucked me away in a small borough in Western Pennsylvania and gave me a porch on which to sit and write with all the time I needed. The latter part took place after my PDD. My daughter was still at home, so she kept me company. I had no other responsibilities to take me away from what God dictated. However, during the darkest periods, God had shined his brightest Light of revelation upon me. The work is an amazing feat in sheer magnitude that was a hallmark of my period of Darkness.

The book is now in print but has not been a runaway best seller. I have learned not to measure success in dollars or popularity. The revelation has a time and season that may still be in the future. For that time, it was a means of healing when I needed it. When the Lord would lead me to a new aspect of the work, it seized me and held me safe for brief periods of time while I pursued the leads. There were times when books would fall off the shelf in bookstores right in front of me; people would leave books laying on tables in reading areas of bookstores or on library tables.

In the process of searching for something else on the Internet, God would place another revelation and get my attention. Sometimes I forget how often he did that and how much time was occupied during that period of Darkness. Those times were when his Light shined the brightest to illumine my path. Even after I moved to Pennsylvania and was unemployed, the Light kept me moving forward.

That one work was not the only writing or ministry I did during PDD. I kept a continual stream of words on paper in my journal. My journal began as thoughts present in my mind; over time I shifted to writing letters to the Lord and those letters became prayers. Later I realized I was writing down what the Lord was saying to me; I was writing the answers to my prayers. In time, I realized that the Lord was also giving me prophesies and was speaking things I had not thought previous to writing them on paper.

I teach writing and I write, so people think writing comes easy to me, but they think they can't do it. That is simply not true unless you do not have hands or unless they do not work well. Even then, there are ways to make writing happen. When most people say they cannot write, they mean that they are afraid to write because of being judged for poor grammar, etc. The good news is that no one but the author reads journals, so it does not matter about grammar, style, or form.

Writing in and through the Darkness is one major way out of Darkness—as I have just said. Sitting quietly with pen and paper puts us in a position to receive words of comfort and healing from God. He wants to be our God and wants us to be his people. All we have to do is show up.

Writing in a journal keeps us busy in a productive way. Previous to picking up the pen, my mind would likely be in a state of chaos or the blanket of fear would have fallen down upon me. Writing enabled me to take the threats and chaos out of my mind and force them into compliance on paper. Putting them on paper organizes my thoughts. Like my confessions, I forced myself to be positive and use faith-filled words, not because I felt that way at the beginning of the writing. These writings were not pity parties, either. They were lines drawn in the sand that put Darkness on notice.

Another means of recovery involved writing in workbooks. The day that my divorce was final, I had to begin a Disciple Study at my church. I thought at first that the timing was bad, but on the day I went to court, I decided it would be an appropriate activity. I was right.

The group involved studying and keeping a workbook daily. While that got me off on the right track immediately, it was Henry Blackaby and Claude King's *Experiencing God* study that held me. I went through the study three times in the course of eighteen months. It is a twelve-week study; each time I went through it, I grew spiritually and moved closer to the end of Darkness.

One additional word about the study: the weekly meetings consisted of watching a short video of Blackaby teaching. He was a gentleman older than I and had a fatherly manner about him. I think in retrospect, his demeanor contributed to my feelings of peace and comfort as I had no living father at the time. Also my husband of 29 years, who had in some ways replaced my fathers, had voluntarily abandoned me, so I needed someone to replace that feeling of security.

The weekly meetings were significant because I was connecting with people, but the workbook exercises gave me a sense of interaction with God as he led me. The time spent reading and responding made the ground under my feet firm and extended the path out of Darkness step by step.

Again, when you pick up pen and paper—cheap and portable tools easy to carry anywhere—you put yourself in a position to receive healing from the Healer himself.

CHAPTER 11

Sacred Healing Art

One of the most regrettable things I did the summer of my divorce was purchase a computerized sewing machine thinking I wanted to produce quilted paintings and textile wall art. Had I known I was not going to be married and would need my money to live, I would not have spent the exorbitant amount on the machine. It really became a luxury when I temporarily lost all of my creativity or the desire to do anything.

Having it, though, I ventured to take it out of the box and learn how to use it. In the process I made a quilted cover for a vanity stool using the various stitches. The activity kept me occupied in addition to giving me a sense of purpose if only for a brief time. It was a very expensive stool cover, though.

I have mentioned elsewhere that writing my book was an outlet with a divine purpose, but I also wrote several poems that would occur to me. Before you turn to another chapter thinking this activity might not be for you, let me remind you that things may be possible coming out of Darkness that might not have been otherwise. Put yourself in a position to receive. Who knows? You might find a hidden talent or a hidden recovery tool.

At one significant point in my walk out, I had been on my porch writing. The sense that I was, indeed, coming through the Darkness occurred to me yet these words came across my mind: "I keep coming to the end of me. . . ." Then I pondered, "which is where I am supposed to be because at the end of me is you."

I stopped what I had been doing at the moment and went to my computer. This is what I wrote once putting my fingers to the keyboard:

I Am

Lord, I keep coming to the end of me,
Which is where I am supposed to be.
For at the end of me there is you.
So today I get out of me and into you
Until the me I am is really you.

It turned out that it was a poem in hiding. I must confess that prior to my dark period, I had only written a couple of what I called poems. In the process of writing them, I learned what poetry is all about. It is a place where the heart goes when it needs to weep (with an audience).

The first real poem I ever wrote came to me after the movie *Awakenings*, the film that is based on a nonfiction book by Dr. Oliver Sacks. The movie is about Dr. Malcolm Sayer's experience with encephalitis patients that had been catatonic in some cases for twenty years. The patients were awakened for a brief period through the drug L-Dopa. The first sign that there was hope for communicating with them was that they responded to certain stimuli. One of those stimuli was playing music that the patient liked; doing so prompted the patients to do some of the perfunctory duties like feeding themselves. This proved to the health care workers that some part of the patients was being affected, that part would be their spirits though their conscious minds slept.

It was a testimony to the separation of spirit and soul. In the end, the L-Dopa lost effect and the patients went back to sleep. The medicine, however, had not been responsible for their responding to their favorite music, which prompted them to do things like feed themselves.

As the movie came to an end, I kept asking, *"Why didn't they keep speaking to their spirits with music?"* I had an intense empathy with the patients. No one is listening to them now. *"That's me,"* I thought. *"I keep 'speaking' within everything I do, but no one is listening—no one is listening."*

I made my way to the car, glad that I had chosen to go to the movie alone. I needed to write my thoughts down. I found a scrap of paper and a pen in the car. I began the trek home thinking I'd write at red lights. As unbelievable as it may be, all 20 or 25 lights were green!

I pulled into my garage and sat in the car as I began to write. After a couple of lines, I realized I was writing a poem, a poem my poet friend said was the saddest thing she had ever heard. That experience occurred about eight years before divorce depression; it expresses the pain I was experiencing in my life, especially in my marriage to someone who was not listening to the cries of my heart. Perhaps we were not listening to each other's cries.

No One is Listening

My spirit needs to speak,
But no one is listening;
My spirit speaks,
But no one is listening;
My spirit speaks their language,
But no one is listening;
My spirit paints for them,
But no one is listening;
My spirit draws for them,
But no one is listening;
My spirit crafts for them,

But no one's listening;
My spirit cooks for them,
But no one's listen'n;
My spirit cries,
But no one's listen'n;
My spirit dies, but no one's listen'n.

Will they miss me
 When my body is here
But my spirit is silent?

As I said, poetry is the place where the heart [spirit] goes when it wants to weep. In that sense, we need to allow that to happen without putting poetry rules upon it. Sit down somewhere even now and let your heart weep. No one has to read or judge what you write.

In the midst of the Darkness, two more poems emerged, each from a single thought. They came from the place where my heart wept to bring healing to two painful events. One was my son's leaving home, a natural occurrence, and my husband's moving into his [the son's] vacated room—which was the first stage of his leaving me. The second was the morning my husband actually moved out with all of his belongings—never to return on a permanent basis again. Although the poems were extremely sad, even to this day, those momentary ventures when Darkness turned to Light made my days a little lighter for having released the pain.

Two years after the writing of those poems when I was well healed and out of the Darkness, I had the privilege of being in England at a World Congress of Poets with American poet Donald Hall, who later became the Poet Laureate of the United States. In a video made that week, Hall talks about the poetry he wrote after his wife, poet Jane Kenyon, had died less than a year before. He said he did not know what people do who do not write poetry. He wrote poetry through his grief. Through her illness and the stages of physical decline, Jane Kenyon had written many poems, which were published after her death. Hall read many of those poems at the Congress.

Whether one is writing through grief or through some other personal trauma, writing of any kind is cathartic, but poetry has the added benefit in that it allows the poet to express emotions in a controlled fashion that can withstand public scrutiny rather than living in a journal or diary. Poetry, like most art forms, seems to demand audience interaction. As I said before, poetry is the place the soul goes to weep.

Writing or anything creative comes from a deep place. Unlocking those deep places is a matter of revelation, I believe. Shortly before the divorce, when I was already in a deep place of grief, I had discovered the art of mandalas while visiting the Great Smoky Mountains. The book I purchased one afternoon intrigued me. I sat in the middle of the motel bed and tried out this art form that the author used as art therapy. At a later time when I was under emotional pressure on the way to the mountains with the family, I drew a few more that expressed deep pain. This event occurred before the divorce and signaled my ongoing pain in a relationship I was holding onto, a relationship that was slowly smothering me—even my soul.

I was on spring break from my college classes when I discovered the mandala painting. When I returned to school, I was scheduled to teach creative writing. The thought occurred to me that this art form could be inspirational in a creative writing environment. I took those thoughts back to class and incorporated the mandalas in my syllabus. There were some amazing results, but one is paramount.

One of the youngest students in the class was going through deeply emotional issues involving some significant people in her life. Her parents had spent a great deal of money on therapists and medication. The writing she had turned in that quarter was not especially impressive and, for the most part, immature because she seemed too preoccupied. That had been the spring quarter.

Midsummer, there was a knock on my door. It was the young student and her mother. I invited them in and they hastened to tell me the purpose of their visit. The student handed me a stack of circle drawings/paintings she had done since spring quarter. She had a sparkle in her eyes that I had not seen in class. Both she and her mother confessed to the remarkable change that had taken place in the student, much greater than anything she had gained from going to the professionals. I cannot take any credit for that except that I introduced her to the concept.

Another amazing story happened to one of the nontraditional students. Mary, not her actual name, was in her forties and was sitting next to me the day the students shared their stories from the mandalas. The assignment was to draw a mandala and write a story that "it" might suggest. Mary was the last one to read.

Her story was about a fifteen-year-old girl whose father had died. She sat on her bed and looked at a mandala on the wall that she had painted after a day in the park with her dad. She became angry at him for dying and leaving her alone. As Mary got to this part, she choked up and so did the rest of the class. She paused to regain her composure but finally handed it to me to finish.

We all sat tearfully awaiting Mary's comments: "I had no idea until just now that this story is about me. I had no idea I was harboring the anger toward my father for dying. I think I am ready to release him now."

There is no telling how much pain Mary might have experienced in her life without knowing why. Her spirit knew but just needed a place and time to reveal it. That class and that drawing put her in the place of opportunity. Find your space and put yourself in a position to receive.

I add these stories and this information here so that you can try it. It may be at the very least one of the diversions I mentioned previously. I will explain how to use the drawings and you can try them. If you would like to see mine, you may go to my website: www.dellbelew.com/Inspirational_Mandalas.html

* * * * * * * *

Before I continue, let me give my disclaimer: I am a Christian and the practice of creating these circle paintings does not conflict with the Word or with my theology. Neither this nor any aspect of this web site is dedicated to nor influenced by Eastern religious practices.

An inspirational mandala is a painting within a circle. The circle can actually be filled in with almost any medium or design, including, as you will see on my website, photography. The most important technical aspect of painting or filling in the circle is that it should most likely be spontaneous in order to be inspirational, although there is no hard and fast rule. I use this concept in classes for self-discovery, recovery, spirituality, creative writing, spiritual centering, and painting. It is an excellent means of free expression and makes artists of everyone. The results are almost always beautiful and surprising.

Being a professor in English and Humanities, I have taught the history of art, music, and literature. This one expressive experience became a culmination of cultural ideas that ultimately revealed how art has recorded the psyche of cultural changes. Along with my own experience, I firmly believe that Art has the power to reveal hidden mysteries of the human spirit, in addition to being a culture's legacy.

Back to my story about discovering mandalas. My spirit craves trees and their life-enriching foliage, which is why I had headed for the mountains of Tennessee during one spring break. I needed the solitude and the quiet sanctity of trees, rocks, and rushing water. But, silly me, I forgot that new northern foliage comes later than in the deep south. I was extremely disappointed when I saw the leafless trees still lingering alongside the mountain road and felt the nippy air of winter. Not to be completely exasperated, I went to my favorite art bookstore and found the aforementioned book. *Creating Mandalas,* by Suzanne Fincher, fascinated me because of the title; then the photos inside sold the book.

I went back to my motel room and began to read. I had acquired some felt-tipped markers and a drawing tablet and decided to try my hand. Being an artist, I thought, would hinder me from free expression. When I finished filling in the white space, I turned the mandala around somewhat and found what I thought was the right position. In the drawing, I found a tree with a landscape and skyscape behind it. I liked what I saw, but I had no immediate sense of what it meant; it didn't need to mean anything.

Because I was going to teach Creative Writing during spring quarter, I thought mandalas might be an interesting means of inspiration. I had forgotten my resolution until the first day of class. As I was discussing the syllabus, it occurred to me to share my experience with mandalas. I ended up assigning a mandala with an accompanying story.

The next day I took my first mandala to show the class. One of my students pointed out that my spirit wanted leaves, so it painted a tree with leaves! She was absolutely right. Based on the position I was making my marks, there had been no semblance of a tree or any recognizable object. The students were amazed at their own discoveries and points of incredible inspiration and many continue to this day to engage in mandala painting.

Thus began my interest in the spiritual power of circle paintings. God can speak through anything as long as we submit ourselves to him and put ourselves in a position to "see." Many such experiences are interwoven through my past during a period of self-discovery and inner healing, which I now share with anyone who wants to listen. I learned more about mandalas as time went by; I used them to paint during the worship service later in Pittsburgh.

"Mandala" in Sanskrit means "circle." In some cultures and religions, it means "sacred or magical" circle because of its spiritual power for unlocking mysteries and interacting with the Divine Spirit. The art of inspirational mandalas represents the point of centering in life that invites the sacred presence of God in a visual way. Then the visual expression speaks Divine secrets back to the artist as well as the beholder.

The process of creating the mandala is of utmost importance because of God's freedom to reveal himself. The product emerges as a community experience whereby the audience engages in the energy of the completed work. As the work provides revelation, it lives in an eternal state for all those who meditate upon it. The spontaneous creations happen before my eyes and give new meaning to the expression, "A picture is worth a thousand words." The sheer joy that comes from these creations heals in areas that I never knew were wounded. Perhaps this is what Solomon meant when he wrote, "A merry heart does good like a medicine" (Pr 17.22).

After I had completed my appointment to the three churches, I found a church whose Bishop encouraged creativity during worship. I later began painting these circle paintings during the worship service. As I had learned before, they had spiritual, even prophetic significance to the congregation watching them unfold (materialize.)

In that church, I also painted clouds on 2,000 square feet of wall space behind the pulpit and choir that also seemed to be anointed. I suspect the anointing came as a result of doing the painting often on a scaffold during worship and in an anointed sanctuary even when it was empty except for me—physically, that is. The clouds, like the mandalas, were subjective and, therefore, open to interpretation. They also gave the people in the sanctuary an opportunity to interpret what the Lord was saying to them.

The psychoanalyst Carl Jung used the mandala in therapy because of its "movement towards psychological growth, expressing the idea of a safe refuge, inner reconciliation and wholeness" and what he termed "individuation." From my own experience in working with mandalas, I found that they reveal something of our spiritual understanding and provide a vessel for God to speak things in colorful language that our minds cannot express in words. Through the meditation of our works, however, we find expressive and beautiful words. Thus, the circle painting is one language communicated from the Divine Spirit to the human spirit.

The information above led ultimately to the Painting in the Spirit ministry. Because I have been called as a prophet and because of the ministry that has evolved, I called myself "The Painting Prophet," and you will see why if you check out my web site and the page marked "Painting in the Spirit." It is certainly better than the weeping or naked prophets of old! And much more joyful and colorful, which I hope you will agree. www.dellbelew.com/painting_in_the_spirit.htm

CHAPTER 13

The Music of Our Spheres

The power of music is undeniable, whether for good or evil. When King Saul was vexed with an evil spirit, he called upon the psalmist David to come and play his harp. When David played, the evil spirit departed. The spirit realm certainly responds to music. For this reason, it is important that we choose the right music when we are in Darkness.

Music not only stirs the soul, it also educates. When children need to learn the alphabet, we teach them the "Alphabet Song." There are numerous musical jingles that are apt to go through our minds in a given day that we have heard in television or radio advertisements. Because we are learning things even when listening to music, it is also important what we choose to listen to when we are in Darkness.

One day while driving my car, I heard myself singing the Pabst Blue Ribbon beer commercial! *"What am I doing?"* I called an immediate halt to my singing, but the experience taught me about the influence of the music. The commercial had struck a positive cord to an already happy day, so I sang along with the song in my mind. Even before I committed my life to Christ, I didn't like beer, so what other reason would I have for singing that jingle except that some very smart advertiser had hooked it to a happy tune? We are continually sold a rotten bill of goods by their being packaged in a pleasant way. The Greek philosopher, Horace, and Mary Poppins understood that a spoonful of sugar makes the [nasty] medicine go down. Horace believed in "delightful instruction" as the best teaching method, which is a happy thought except for the fact that not everything should be taught!

The reason music has such an effect on us has been the subject of many books and theories. The one most believable to me is Kepler's discovery of the "Music of the Spheres" in what he believes is the very essence of the universe. Before Kepler, Pythagoras, the mathematic philosopher, had done studies about musical harmony, ultimately concluding that the universe is constructed of certain rhythms that formed chords and regular chord lengths. Interestingly, Pythagoras' followers used music in healing of body and soul.

We do not need to be scientists or philosophers to know that music has the power to heal or stir emotions; we learn this by experience. The rhythms of nature harmonize with our bodies and, thus, our souls. The rhythm of our bodies is another aspect that is affected by the Darkness of depression. I believe our essential rhythms remain the same and determine our personalities, but they are adjustable depending on outward and inward stimuli.

In my period of Darkness, music caused my physical body to respond based solely on the memories it stirred. Music, as a result, became obviously soulish (mental). The soul is defined as the mind, will, and emotions, so I had control over the way it affected my emotions.

When I was out in public or at someone else's house, I could not control the music or the effect it had on me. However, I could willfully choose how I would respond. My usual response was to flee, to leave the building. To remain would bring on more emotions that I was working hard to control until they could be healed.

My root cause of depression was the breaking up of my family and the disconnection from all that was "familiar" or "familial." My friend, Laurie, had told me, "When your world falls down around you, make another one." Before I could build a new one, I had to keep the old one from sabotaging me at every turn. I learned quickly that music was the most powerful conductor of the old life.

I had liked Southern gospel music and traditional hymns of the Church, but so did my former husband. When I heard that music, the connections to him and my old life caused me to fall back into the black hole. The sad commentary on that is church music should have been inspirational and should have reminded me of God's provision. For a time, I had to tune it out. I attended a church that played more contemporary choruses; I had tapes of that kind of music that filled the space in my car with the same. That was the music of my new life and it filled my soul with hope and courage.

Later I knew I was healed when I could hear the former without fleeing. Country music had been another favorite genre, but so many of those lyrics involve cheating, drinking, and loneliness. They definitely had to go! And so they did. Each person going through Darkness must decide which forms of music affect which parts of her soul. Run *to* the inspirational and *from* the devastating.

There was one that became my "fight song": "Shut up and Drive" by Cheley Wright. The story of the music video said it all; a woman, who is driving away from her possibly unfaithful lover, watches him in the rearview mirror obviously saddened by the leaving. Her mirror speaks up and says, "Shut up and drive. You'll only miss the man you wanted him to be." These were words and images I needed to hear. Temporarily they would boost my ego and make me believe it was up to me whether that would be the best or worst days of my life. The resounding message was "move on . . . ." And I did.

Thirteen years after my PDD, I had another brief bout with Darkness; this time unrelated to another human being, but the methods for breakthrough were the same. That depression, as mentioned before, was medically induced. I did not have the same reactions to music; but, strangely and mysteriously, music died for me. Even now I rarely listen to music when I have a choice. I listen to cable news, talk radio, or teaching. I cannot say why; perhaps I never fully recovered from the impact of music in Darkness. It may very well be the fact that my ministry/calling is teaching that I gravitated toward talk rather than music. I have to work on that because music is important and connects me to the universe, as I have been saying here.

One example of the effect of music occurred when I was in a department store with my daughter. I was on one side of the store in my department and she was on the other in hers. The music playing in the store was the Oldies from my era. I had not paid much attention at first, but one song got my attention suddenly and I felt a dramatic shift in my mood. I simply shuttered and let out a low groan. The groan implied I needed to go home right that moment or I might explode. Suddenly with that thought, my daughter appeared, "Is it that depression again?"

"Yes," I replied, "and I need to go home." I held back the tears until I got home and could get in my sacred place. When I got home, I headed straight for my prayer closet. I fell on my knees and cried out loudly to God for help.

I am not sure how I could advise anyone to respond to music because each of us reacts differently. My chief advice, as with other factors, listen to your own spirit, soul and body and feed it only what leads to positive, faith-filled, and hopeful outcomes. On occasion people in the Darkness resort to "crying-in-your-beer" music; to do so is to bring on more misery. Trust me. Recovery demands that we turn from self-pity and those pitiful parties. Move on! Guard your spirit against sudden attacks that will bring you down rather than out. Choose to listen to what feeds your soul good food and spit out the rotten stuff before your soul becomes contaminated.

One last example of the power of music to heal happened outside of my dark period but is indelibly marked on my mind. I owned a hair salon and had decided to sell out because I was attending college and wanted to go full time. I had told my customers to start looking for another hairdresser.

Within a week of that decision, I came down with a low-grade temperature that lasted a couple of days. There were no other symptoms, so I had no idea why it was hanging on. I kept moving forward and taking care of business until the third day when the fever rose and sapped my strength to the point where I had to stop.

I had a music tape with instrumental praise music, so I turned it on and lay down on the sofa. As I closed my eyes, I saw myself walking on the side of a mountain. In the next scene, Jesus met me and offered me a seat on a large flat rock. Once I was seated, he spoke, "I did no tell you to sell your shop."

"Well, ok!" I jumped up and started calling my clients to tell them not to find a new hairdresser because I was not selling the salon. By the time I was finished calling, I realized my fever was gone and my strength was restored. My fever had gotten my attention, so the Lord could speak. The praise music was the vehicle that brought the Lord on the scene. I had not purposely conjured up the event; Christ had literally shown up with the word of knowledge about my decision. It was a couple of years before I got the release to sell it. In the meantime, one of my Spirit-filled friends needed a salon in which to work. Her working there solved both of our needs; she worked the business when I was not there so

I was able to attend school full-time. The Lord met both of our needs, but he could not have if I had sold the business out of season. When the time was right, I sold it and kept a salon in my house, which I had had before, in order to pay for my education.

Like it did for me that particular day, the music of the spheres bridges the gap between God and his children. The Scriptures say that God inhabits the praises of his people (Ps 22.3). If you want to bring him on the scene and activate his Divine Light, praise him; doing so in music brings the entire universe into harmony with you and in submission to him. It just doesn't get any better than that!

The Dark Side of Darkness

U p until this point, I have stressed the fact that the only way out of Darkness is the Light of Jesus Christ that he shines upon our path. He pierces the Darkness of our darkest days. I have also stressed the importance of knowing ourselves and our enemy. The process by which we do both can be brief or painfully drawn out, as was the case with my PDD. Though I do not wish that on anyone, the end result is freedom from not only depression but the deep seated corners of the dark sides that are hidden even from ourselves.

Everyone has these dark corners, but some keep them hidden better than others. Sadly, the deeper they are hidden the more external affect they have upon us; in almost all deeply hidden corners there is a wick on the end of a stick of dynamite that stands near an open flame getting ready to explode.

The dark side of the human spirit and soul is the fallen nature, or the sin nature. Paul's admonishment for us to "save" ourselves comes from our need to examine all of our passages leading to those corners. Jesus' blood was more than sufficient to purchase our eternal life and reconcile us to God when we surrender to him and confess our fallen state. Our flesh, our carnal nature, tends to rebel.

Every human is born with the propensity to commit sin, so even when we are born again of the Spirit, our carnal man needs to be renewed. We do this by renewing our minds with the Word of God and by opening our minds so that the Light of Christ can reveal hidden motives, pains, memories, and even words spoken over us that pierced our tender spirits when we were too young to understand.

I will hasten to say this is not some hocus-pocus, psycho babble, or new age philosophy. There was a teaching thirty or forty years ago referred to as "healing of the memories," which was popularized by Jimmy Carter's sister, Ruth Carter Stapleton. It is a dangerous teaching when the practitioner probes too deeply and for too long. It borders on the psychic and opens the door to the enemy forces standing ready to intensify the process and lead the "patient" into deeper corners of darkness. When we commit our way to the Lord and cover our minds with the blood of Christ, we hear from him when the time for deliverance is right. Probing, as such, is not necessary but discernment is.

There are other ways that one can open the door to the enemy. One seemingly harmless one is the Ouija board. Going to fortune tellers or psychics or calling the psychic hotlines are viewed, especially in our culture, as fun and games so they are engaged innocently enough; however, they not only invite the enemy in but they also enter into his playground. That is a dangerous place because his equipment is booby-trapped and designed to steal, kill, and destroy. In the book of Deuteronomy 18.9-14, God forbids such activity for very good reason and it behooves us to pay attention.

Let us look at the first place Jesus went after he was baptized by John and before he began his earthly ministry. If a man like Jesus who was not born in sin and was not tempted by sin had to face the enemy straightaway, how much more should we? Satan pulled out all of the stops and tempted Jesus in ways that most of us will never be; Jesus fought the enemy with the same weapons that he gave us to use, the Word of God. In an earlier chapter, I explain how God used his Word in awesome ways to help me fight the good fight of faith both offensively and defensively. Do not forget from the experience of Jesus in the wilderness that Satan knows the Word, too, but he will misquote it—partly to trap you and partly because he does not understand the spiritual implications. Jesus did and he was able to withstand all the fiery darts of the wicked one and showed us how.

The corners of darkness can also be referred to as strongholds. The only one who can see into those corners and break the strongholds is the Holy Spirit. Because he knows what is in our hearts [spirits] and knows when we are ready to be released, he moves in his divine wisdom and timing. Timing is everything. We must surrender our wills to be delivered, but he shines the Light in the dark corner.

On one occasion during my porch time, I was listening to a tape of a service in which Bob Mumford, well-known Bible teacher at the time, was giving his testimony. Another person was praying over him and had a word of knowledge said, "Lord, Bob has lost his little boy."

By that I thought maybe he was grieving over the loss of a son. Listening further, I realized what she meant was that he had lost his childhood due to his father's death at a young age when he still had children and a wife to support. The responsibility for taking care of the family fell on Bob who was much too young for the task. It became clear to Mumford that he had been grieving his entire adult life about this loss of childhood.

As I listened, I suddenly realized something from my own infancy and said over and over, "It was not my fault. It was not my fault."

"Why in the world was I saying that?" I kept asking myself. The Lord showed me that even as an infant our human spirits can pick up and be influenced by words and emotions happening around us. I had been conceived out of wedlock and born into a "good Baptist" family for which this was shameful. No doubt there was much negative talk and grief over my birth, though I can say I was much loved by my mother and her family.

However, at the moment of that revelation, the Lord showed me that one of my dark corners was the shame I carried even though *it was not my fault*. Once the shame came up, I renounced it and the stronghold was broken. That was my time and timing is everything. That was one of the many strongholds broken during my PDD. The Truth was setting me free one step at a time.

Although the release of strongholds is a means of spiritual healing, it is not the only one by far. I recall telling a friend who was also going through depression that I had on one occasion told the spirit of depression to go in Jesus' name.

"Oh, depression is a spirit?" was her reply.

"Yes," I responded, "and you should rebuke it." It was then I realized that most people are not aware of Satan's part in depression. I have spent many pages explaining the means by which I traveled light out of Darkness, but spiritual warfare is one of the less practiced methods people use.

Not every moment of sadness or depression is caused directly by an evil spirit. Nor is every depression the result of demonic activity. Because I am not a scientist, I will not venture to explain the ins and outs of the psychological aspects, though I am an expert on the way the Darkness behaves. Even with psychological causes, I feel pretty certain there is an evil spirit prodding. I felt like Satan had turned me every which way but loose. Sometimes he was more obvious than others in his approach. Sometimes I praised the Lord and drove him out; sometimes through revelation, the Lord released him; and sometimes I just rebuked him in Jesus' name.

While I don't look for demons under every rock, I do not discount the Holy Spirit's ability to give me discernment. One lady in my writing group said she believed in the devil, but some of her friends did not. I told her the next time the subject comes up, she should remind them that Satan believes in them and is very much aware of their existence. Satan's job is to steal, kill, and destroy us. Some people make his job easy. They pretend he isn't there, which is really bad news for them.

Sadness, anxiety, panic, grief, and fear are demonic spirits. If you can name it, there is a very good possibility it is a demonic spirit. As mentioned before, I was in a constant state of sadness and grief for more than eighteen months with only brief periods of relief. Then there were unannounced moments when I felt as if a blanket fell over me when everything in my surroundings turned gray—literally. I could not see clearly nor could I see color. Color requires light and, though I could see daylight, all of the color was washed out of my world during those times, momentary though they were most of the time.

Those were times when Satan would turn up the intensity. Those were the times I would put into action all that I knew to do. Those were the moments when the spirit of fear would show up. Fear is an evil task master that can come in many forms from covert to overt expressions. The effects can be devastating, especially if you do not know it is coming or what to do with it when it does.

Gerald Derstine, a well-known Bible teacher back in the 70s and 80s wrote a book about demonic activity. I am sorry that I cannot recall the title. He explained the process of possession like this: It begins with depression, then goes to obsession and finally to possession. The stages intensify as each gets more serious and as each takes greater control of one's life. This would be reason enough to counteract the effects of depression right away.

No matter what the degree of your depression, Jesus wants you to be free to experience his joy. My first and best suggestion is that you study the scriptures concerning spiritual warfare. Jesus and others had much to say about the subject. The place of Satan in the world and his intentions for Christians come through the events recorded in Revelation 12. That chapter tells how Satan came to be our enemy and why he works so diligently to destroy us.

Throughout the Old Testament, we can see the efforts to destroy the woman and her seed, especially the covert actions to destroy Israel, the root and offspring of Jesus and all of those who came after him. This subject is the thesis of my previous book, *The Woman, The Red Dragon, and The End of the Age*, about which I was actively writing during my Darkness. The book may be on some level the root reason or the very cause for my Darkness (PDD) so as to keep me from sharing the revelation of the book. Though I shamelessly plug my book here, I do so because the information is pertinent to the battle between God and Satan over the dominion of the earth; and Satan's wrath for the Woman and her Seed and God's protection of his people. You can get a copy of my book from Amazon.com or Barnes and Noble.com, but the best place is through my website because it is less expensive: www.dellbelew.com.

Nevertheless, an informed audience is forearmed. Knowledge of the enemy's devices is both offensive and defensive. When you learn who he is and how he operates, you can see him coming and defend yourself. Please be warned, as Paul warned us, that the devil knows if you do not know your authority in the name of Jesus. It is a matter of faith. Read about the sons of Sceva in Acts 19. Among the crowd when Paul was casting out demons were "vagabond Jews" who were exorcists. When they saw Paul healing the sick and casting out demons in Jesus' name while ministering in Ephesus, they called out people who had evil spirits and commanded them in the name of "Jesus whom Paul preacheth" (19.13).

They got a response but not the one they expected: "the evil spirit answered and said, 'Jesus I know, and Paul I know; but who are you?'" (19.15) With that the evil spirit jumped upon the sons of Sceva and "overcame them" (i.e., beat them up), so that they fled out of the house naked and wounded" (19.16). So if you do not wish to get beaten to a pulp and sent out naked, say what you mean and mean what you say in dealing with evil spirits. The good news about the story: the word was spread abroad about what happened to the exorcists and the fear of God fell upon the people and the Lord Jesus was magnified" (19.17). They brought all of their "curious arts" and books and burned them up to be rid of all that was related to evil spirits and their activity. (These books and arts would include things they used to conjure up spirits—like modern day Ouija boards, tarot cards, and the like.)

As I said before, if you have had any part in anything that smacks of psychic phenomenon, whether for "fun" or guidance, renounce it right now in Jesus' name. Taking part in such things gives Satan license to wreck your lives in one way or the other.

Another important aspect of spiritual warfare is to submit yourself to God, resist the devil, and he will flee from you (James 4.7). I am constantly amazed at how many people will resist the reality that Satan exists or that he has anything to do with their depression or physical illness before they resist Satan. To me, it is much easier and more profitable to believe this and cast it out than fight the Darkness on my own. This is war and surrender is not an option.

Psychotherapy, Counseling, and Medication

My doctorate is in English, so I do not presume to give medical advice of any kind. Although I do pastoral counseling, I am not offering advice in an official capacity either. I am strictly testifying to my own experience and what worked for me. So, please regard what I am about to say as merely suggestions. Seek help from a trained medical profession before taking or discontinuing medication.

I begin with the easy part. After a few days of crying constantly and cajoling my husband to reconsider, I knew I needed help beyond myself in the form of a pastoral counselor. My own pastor at the time would have seen me on a regular basis, but he often dozed in the one or two sessions I had with him. So much for that.

After asking around, I learned of a Christian counseling ministry in town that did not charge a fee. When I called, I was given an appointment the day before my court date. "*Too late,*" I thought, but I held on until that day. There had been a mix up and instead of meeting with a female (their policy), I had a male counselor. That turned out to be good for me because he was able to give me the male perspective and help me stay hopeful and grounded. I saw the Christian counselor nearly every week for two years.

While I highly recommend counseling, I do so with a note of hesitation. Not all Christian counselors are truly Christian nor are they all equipped with the best counsel. Do the research and choose carefully. By all means, pray about where to go or whom to see.

I have mentioned previously that the Disciple Study and Experiencing God group studies had helped me tremendously not only because of the group meeting but also the workbooks that gave me an activity during the week to direct my attention away from my present emotional pain. Another group that I joined during that time was DivorceCare. I have since become a Group Leader. These groups, of course, are relative to divorce support while the others are for individuals who want to grow in spirituality and who are not necessarily depressed. You can get information on the web just by typing in DivorceCare. I highly recommend it for the group interaction, the workbook, and the videos designed for specific topics each week that consist of teaching and personal testimonies of people who have gone through divorce—and survived.

As to the psychotherapy, psychiatrists, and psychologists, I can only say be very careful. Some of them went into their fields because they need help themselves. [Not being funny necessarily. We are all flawed in some way.] I have a few friends who seem no better off than if they had not gone to professionals. It all boils down to two things: 1) seek advice from the one who created you; and 2) pay attention to do what you are told. Simply going to a session every week to vent or look for pity and then walk away the same as you went in is a waste of time, money, and life. (The same is true for this book; if you paid anything for this and do not take advantage of the advice offered, you have wasted your money and time.)

Another area for caution is medicine, antidepressants, which are the drugs of choice for depression. When life gets unbearable for any reason, the average human reaches for the medicine bottle. Until I went into Darkness, I had no idea how many people are on antidepressants and have been for many years—many of them don't seem very steady or less depressed.

Having never been a pill person and having heard all the reports about the side effects of Prozac, especially the fact that it caused some people to commit suicide, pills were out of the question for me. I particularly resisted any mind-altering drugs. I was not happy in my own thoughts, but I could still have control over them. Then one day when I had an emotional melt-down after class, I called my doctor to see if he could work me in. Seeing the emotional state I was in, he grabbed his prescription pad and wrote one for Prozac, the very drug I was afraid to take. What was even worse was that it would be weeks before the drug took effect, but I needed help right then.

I began that afternoon, reluctantly. Within 24 hours my tongue began to swell. Once I realized what was happening, I called the doctor. He told me to quit taking the pills immediately and take Benedryl for the allergic reaction. In fact, I believe what was happening was that my body was rejecting the drug due to my fear of it. The doctor called in another antidepressant for me to "try."

Again, I took the pills reluctantly. The next day in class as my students were writing, I sat quietly and graded essays. Suddenly, in my stillness, I felt a strange sensation at the base of my skull like something was squeezing and releasing that part of my brain. The feeling was frightening.

I pledged not to try another antidepressant. They seemed to be adding to my Darkness and not helping. One thing I did learn from the allergic reaction to Prozac was that Benedryl worked and did so immediately. It became my drug of choice, especially for anxiety attacks. Although Benedryl usually makes people drowsy, I found that the drowsy effect enabled me to come down from the heightened emotions caused by the anxiety attack. In another chapter, I mention a trip to Atlanta that I had to take. It was Benedryl that calmed me down once I got to the conference. I took a Benedryl sometimes at night if I could not settle down. Like other over-the-counter drugs, however, regular use tends to make them ineffective.

Shifting from the PDD to the later period of depression precipitated by blood pressure medication, let me say that I talked to several friends who were on Zoloft without harmful effects or dependency. I did decide to try it, but like most of them, it took a few weeks to take effect. There were some early effects that were unpleasant and by the time they were well into my system, the depression lifted due in large part to having found the correct blood pressure medication for me. After a few months, I slowly discontinued the Zoloft. (Oddly, one medication's side effects forced me into another—neither of which did I want to take.)

My stories are just that, MY stories. I hate to be dependent upon medication of any kind, so it is not surprising that I had so little results. The best advice I can give is to take Jesus 24/7. He is a habit you will not want to break, and there are no harmful side effects. We are fearfully and wonderfully made and our Creator knows how to fix what is broken.

CHAPTER 15

Prayer and Sovereignty

The absolute most important aspect of walking out of Darkness is prayer. Although I have already discussed prayer in conjunction with everything else in my traveling Light, I would be remiss if I did not call specific attention to the matter. The reason this short chapter is important is that prayer is the essence of my connection to the Father of Light.

His divine presence abides in me, walks beside me, goes before me, and guards me from behind by the Holy Spirit. He knew me intimately before I was conceived; he ushered me into this life; he knows every thought before I think it; he sits where I sit, and walks where I walk; he is already in places I will be in the future; and he knew my end before my beginning. None of that has changed. Nothing I go through is a surprise to him and there is nothing that he cannot handle or see me through.

So what am I saying about prayer? Every day of my life, every word I speak, and every thought I think is my prayer. No matter whether I bow my head, look up to heaven, close my eyes, get on my knees, fall on my face, or fold my hands, *he is aware*.

Why, then, are we admonished to pray without ceasing, pray fervently, or shout to the Lord with a loud voice? Why should we follow the example of Jesus and others? The reason is simple: *we need to be aware* of his presence, his promises, and his provisions.

Practically speaking, if we need a simple formula for praying, we can use the four aspects of prayer that follow the sequence of the acronym ACTS.

A is for adoration: we adore him because he is the Almighty. Adoration acknowledges who he is and brings him on the scene. I know I have already said that he is here, but he manifests himself when we adore him. "God inhabits the praises of his people." At the same time, we are reminding ourselves of his almighty power to save, heal, and deliver us.

The C is confession that puts us in our place as we acknowledge our own faults and shortcomings. Then, when we forgive others, Christ forgives us and cleanses us of our unrighteousness and puts us back in right standing with the Father (1 John 1.9.) Confession and forgiveness bridge the gap between us and the throne of heaven.

Once we are forgiven, the T for thanksgiving is the natural outcome as we acknowledge our gratitude for all we are and all we have, which comes to us because of his grace and mercy. We do nothing to deserve either. Paul says, "In everything give thanks for this is the will of God in Christ Jesus concerning you" (I Thes 5.18).

Supplication, the S, is the part of prayer when we can approach our Father who sits on the throne of grace because of the redemptive work at Calvary and make our needs and wants known. When our supplication is for others, we approach the throne boldly and receive not only for the others but for ourselves. Beyond that point of asking, the redemptive work of Christ means that there are things that we do not even need to ask for because they have already been given to us freely, though they cost Jesus everything—a great price! This is the time in prayer where we need to know what Christ has done for us, what he expects from us, and what his will is for us. So we don't have to ask but believe that we receive. He tells us if we ask anything in his name according to the will of the Father, he will give it to us. The only hard part and the part where we get stuck is knowing God's will.

His promises are many so we can make a withdrawal anytime without asking but by giving thanks. This is the reason I started my walking prayer with, "I thank you, Lord, that _____ " and filled in the blanks with promises in his Word. By telling him, I was reminding myself and building up my faith.

The place where prayers of supplication become cloudy and difficult is the specific circumstances about directions for our individual lives—e.g., what man we will marry, what job, what house, and thousands of other "whats" and wants. I am sure that redemption's [salvation] price has been paid and the doors opened for healing, new birth, and deliverance from death, hell, and the grave. The Father's perfect will in EVERYTHING is for my good.

That's being said, let me explain one of the monumental revelations I received in my prayer closet: the sovereignty of God. I had been before PDD adamant about what God would and would not do in my life to the point where I would jump to his defense when anyone would accuse him of something dastardly.

Often when something that I was believing for God to do did not happen, I would blame the people making the decision or the devil. I learned in the Darkness, however, that the circumstances in my life are directed by God, and he puts obstacles before us to keep us on the right path. When the right things happened, he gave me confirmation. I had believed I could have anything I asked for, forgetting the "in God's will" part.

There aren't enough words for me to tell all of the times before and since PDD that I have been disappointed, anxious, and afraid when things went horribly wrong in my circumstances after I prayed. Let me hasten to say that failure to let our requests be known to God is not right either.

Later, when I would see the Lord's hand in the situations actually protecting me from getting off of the track and onto a dangerous road that might have led to ruin, I was grateful for unanswered prayer. This revelation held me through the valley of Darkness as I came to see the Light manifested in my life. I cannot say to this day exactly what God was up to in my PDD, but he was up to something that did and is working not only for my good but for the good of others with whom I have come in contact. I have known many benefits from God's redirecting me sixteen years ago, but others I will not know till I pass over into Eternity.

One benefit I pray will come of my traveling Light in times of Darkness is that others reading this book and hearing my testimony will walk out of the Darkness and into his marvelous Light. Amen

CHAPTER 16

Traveling Connections

A lthough I have saved this information for the last, I do so because it is most important in the list of activities. I want it to stick in your memory like the spices in your mouth and the satisfied feeling after a good meal, a kind of spiritual aftertaste.

My relationship to God in the intimate moments of my walk through Darkness was vital to shore up my spirit, but the interaction with the body of Christ gave me courage and the sense of connectedness. While the Scriptures tell us to "'forsake not the assembling of ourselves together,'" many of us tend to turn away from church at the first sign of trouble; many even turn away from God while we are shaking our fists at him. This should not be. We need each other in our battles because we are told that one can put a thousand [of our enemies] to flight but two can put ten thousand to flight. When we just double our attack weapons, we can create a thousand times the results. That would seem to be the most significant reason to join forces with other believers.

Now, who is it we are putting to flight? The enemies of our souls—spirit beings who mean to steal, kill, and destroy us, evil spirits. Our battles are not with flesh and blood but with spirits of Darkness and wickedness. Remember that those are the same enemies that war or battle against our enemies in the flesh. I was not the only one hurting or being devastated by my depression. To fight off those real enemies we need to join forces with other believers. Whenever two or three are gathered together in Christ's name, he is there in force! Also, and very importantly, God inhabits—lives, dwells—in the praises of his people. When we assemble as believers for public worship, God shows up and shows out. This is the most important reason for assembly with other people, but it is certainly not the only one.

In the Church where God is praised and the minister is called, there is an anointing on the Word that is presented. While we can read the Word and God can reveal himself anywhere, the anointing on the preached word is a fulfillment of a promise based on our obedience. See Deuteronomy 28.

What we hear in corporate worship pulls us together and fortifies us for ministry to one another and to the world. Proverbs tells us that before we go to war, we should seek counsel, for in the counsel of many, there is safety (Pr 11.14; 24.6). We are called as the body of Christ to work together for a common purpose: ministry to a lost and dying world. We cannot do that if we are lost and dying in the field of battle or in the cave of Darkness.

This fact gives us a purpose during times of Darkness. The purpose is an activity that takes our minds off of ourselves and points us to the needs of others. James instructs us to pray for others that we might be healed; lay hands on the sick so that they will recover, so that the prayer of faith will save the sick and the Lord will raise him/her up. We should also confess our faults one to another. The fervent prayer of a righteous man or woman avails much. We do this in corporate worship (James 5).

One of the most regrettable aspects of the twenty-first century church is our empty buildings on Sunday and Wednesday evenings. There was a time when buildings were beehives of spiritual activity. Now it seems people do not want their weekends interrupted by too many church activities, especially pastors.

Sorry, did I step on someone's toes? We think that twice on Sunday and again on Wednesday night is just too much for our busy lives. Meanwhile, the church stands empty except for Sunday morning and a few community activities that take place in spaces rented or used for events other than those that edify believers and provide a sanctuary for the wounded or lost. The early church met daily from house to house when they did not have a common place of worship.

When I attended the first meeting of the Disciple group on the day that my divorce was finalized, I thought I might die. Instead, I found that it was a safe place, a place of healing and recovery. I began to look for places to go the other nights of the week. Because I lived in a small town, that was a challenge. Going to church was a large part of my healing as I travelled toward the Light.

I found information from the teaching, friends who lifted me up, opportunities to share not only my prayer needs but also the revelations God was giving me in the midst of Darkness. I took part in recovery groups such as DivorceCare, for which I was a group leader 15 years later. I certainly don't believe God caused me to divorce and go through PDD just so I could be a comfort to others, but I surely wanted to squeeze every ounce of good out of a very bad experience in my life.

I learned that many people go through depression that is often undetected. Because I had been there [in depression], I was sensitive to the signs. One primary example was what happened to a former student. He had written an essay in which he apologized for not attending class. He described his life as barely being able to get out of bed and not wanting to hang out with his friends or do things he previously enjoyed. The red flags went up and I wrote on his paper that this sounded like depression and I asked him if he had seen the campus counselor or had sought a professional opinion.

The student dropped out of school and I never heard from him again that quarter. About six months later, I received a phone call from his father. The father explained that his son had gotten into trouble with a policeman and was going to court in two weeks. After having been arrested for assaulting an officer, the student's parents began to take him to professionals to determine what was happening to him. The professionals determined that he was bi-polar [manic-depressive], which is a condition in which the patient has extreme mood swings from deep depression to great heights of happiness. This bi-polar condition was the defense his attorney was using in court.

That is where I came in. The father was asking me to testify to the note I wrote on the student's paper in which I recognized his depression before he had the run-in with the policeman and before he was diagnosed. While I made sure the attorney knew that my Ph.D. did not qualify me to give expert testimony, I was willing to do anything I could to help my former student. Sadly, I was still in PDD myself at the time, but the case gave me something to occupy my mind and to direct my attention somewhere besides my own problems.

I arrived at the courthouse and met the family. During the time I waited, I was able to witness to the student's parents about the delivering power of Christ. I boldly explained that God was with them, and he would make a way for them to recover. They had spent thousands of dollars on medical bills and legal fees over the case to the point of having to get a second mortgage on their house, which they were just before losing. I knew if God could sustain me through my Darkness, he could do the same for their son and them.

I did not get to the witness stand that day but was told to come back the next. They had not called any of the witnesses, but the attorney was really troubled about what had happened in court that day. I prayed and believed God was with them. I returned the next day and waited in the hall outside the courtroom. After about an hour, their attorney came out and gathered the family together. In a short time, the father came over to explain that the judge had thrown out the case. It seems the district attorney had failed to renew his license for quite some time. All of the cases he had tried had to be overturned because he was practicing law without a license. I did not understand all that meant except that the young man and his parents had been set free! God had stopped the chaos and freed the victims. The timing indicates once again that timing is everything when you are believing God for deliverance.

That one moment of discernment when I read my student's paper had set in motion a miracle of God's provision for something that would take place later. It put me in a position to receive. God showed me once again his power to save and restore. It was a story etched in my life that revealed a ray of Light that said, "I am here and I know where you are every minute of every day."

If God is able to speak to me, to comfort me, and guide me through chaos and Darkness, he can do no less for anyone who calls upon him. I learned that ministry is the natural outgrowth of our own recovery. The anointing carries the Word beyond our personal lives and our church engagements to the dark corners of other people's lives and reveals the way out.

The peace I felt when I was in church was so significant that I had wished I could stay there and sleep on the pew. Every minute I spent in the house of God was a minute closer to total recovery. The most memorable service was in a small town in Georgia about 90 miles from my home. My daughter attended a Christian school at the time. She had asked permission to attend a service there to hear John Kilpatrick, the pastor of Brownsville Assembly of God in Pensacola, Florida. The Brownsville church had been experiencing a mighty move of God for nine months. Hundreds of thousands—maybe millions by then—had flocked to the place where salvation and healing were the daily occurrences. I had not heard of the pastor or the church, but I agreed to go and drive her there.

To my disappointment, she didn't want to ride with me but with her school friends in the church van. Even though I couldn't find anyone to ride with me, I decided to go anyway. I had wrestled with the decision all day. About twenty miles down the road, I had an anxiety attack and turned my van around to go back home. I parked on the side of the road and called my sister.

She did not hesitate when she said, "Turn your van back around and go on, right now." I heard the authority in her voice and did as she said. I arrived early and found a seat and waited for the service to begin. Even in the nearly empty sanctuary, there was a noticeable presence of God. There had been a noon service, so I assumed the Spirit was still lingering there. He was a welcome presence that day.

The excitement and anticipation grew as the sanctuary filled with worshippers. The praise services proved to be one of the most heightened I have every experienced, never mind how much I needed it. The visiting Kilpatrick gave his testimony about the Father's Day service that broke out in revival that had not waned for nine months. As a side note, the church continued for many years in revival. The service I attended that night in Brunswick was Kilpatrick's first speaking engagement outside of his own church, and I was blessed to be there.

Nothing builds faith like hearing the testimony of God's miraculous power working in people's lives. The words Kilpatrick spoke had a visible power. The Scriptures describe God's Word as a two-edged sword, words that divide asunder, words that I had never "seen" before. After his testimony came the demonstration or manifestation of the power and presence of the Holy Spirit in our midst.

At this point, let me say that I am a cautious person and even a skeptic at times about things I witnessed. The power of God, which I watched at a distance, drained the energy from Pastor Kilpatrick to the point that he had two men holding him at the elbow to keep him from falling. It seemed a little theatrical to me, but I watched and waited as he got closer to my area of the sanctuary. The chairs had been removed for greater mobility of the people receiving prayer.

Almost everyone who had been touched by the pastor had fallen; some people call this being "slain in the Spirit." I continued to be skeptical until he was about six feet away from me. Waves of excitement, intense excitement, rushed over me as he got closer. I tried to explain it away, but it was very real, even tangible.

Though I did not succumb right away, the peace of God overwhelmed me and I sat there among many others who either lay or sat on the floor. I have no way of knowing exactly how long I sat there. I had never felt that depth of peace in my life. It was real; it was compelling; and it was healing.

The next night I returned. The presence of God continued to permeate the sanctuary. The praise and worship was vibrant, but the sermon was the most powerful I had ever heard before or since. I had heard the message preached before and knew the story, but the anointing that was upon John Kilpatrick that night brought new life and power to the sermon.

The message was about the treasures of darkness where the enemy [thief] had stored the things he had stolen from believers. The pastor built upon the promise of God that when a thief steals from us, he has to pay us back either twice or up to seven times.

The message built up such excitement in my spirit that I sat upon the end of the chair and cheered. "Yes! Yes!" I kept saying. Here is the most amazing part: I was the only one being so vocal. That never happens with me. I am not very vocal or demonstrative in a church service!

The fact that the enemy had to return seven times what he had stolen from me during my divorce energized me. At the end of the sermon, the congregation prayed and confessed in unison, actually demanded that the enemy give back our stolen items times seven. I did but I soon realized that would mean one husband times seven. *One would be quite enough,* I thought. [On an important side note, in less than a year my ex-husband was back—only one.]

There were numerous highlights in church services and Bible studies through the eighteen months that shed more and more Light upon my life in the Darkness. Another memorable experience involved a service with a prophet from a nearby town. My friend had been to the church in our town that morning and suggested I go to hear him that evening.

My skepticism included prophecies, but I was open to hear. "[I]n the mouth of two or three witnesses is every word established" is a maxim I hold to when it comes to someone presuming to speak for God (2 Cor 13.1). I believe that God still speaks through people today, but I am on the lookout for the witness of my spirit for discernment.

The service was at a relatively small church, so there was standing-room only. Before the preacher finished his message, he walked over to me and said, "Sister, the Lord has anointed you to bring healing to a man with serious heart trouble, I mean serious heart trouble. God wants to heal him."

"What did that mean?" I wondered. The word was much longer than that, but I hoped upon hope that it had something to do with my ex although he did not have heart trouble—not the

physical kind anyway. The man with heart trouble did emerge one year later and it was not my ex; that is a story for another book. At the moment, the word gave me hope and something for which to look forward. The prophet came back to me later and gave me more hope, "The best years of your life are on you and ahead of you." Good words indeed. I clung to them for many years after they were spoken and after I had walked out of Darkness. As I write them now, I feel hope and joy arise in me.

Every word of the prophet's revelation has come to pass: this is the proof of the spirit of a prophet. The man with serious heart trouble, though he has had several close calls, continues to thrive fourteen years later. The lesson in that evening's experience is that we must put ourselves in a position or place to receive from God whether it is a miracle, a healing, a revelation, or a word of prophecy. That place can be anywhere, but it is likely not going to be in the bed with the cover pulled over your head in fear or in a bottle.

The one reason I know this is because getting your head straight and getting your life back on track require that you first know that depression is caused in part or carried on by becoming disconnected; it could be a disconnect from a person or a thing, like a job or a house.

I learned early in my depression that the greatest threat to my security and sanity was being disconnected. When I speak of connection I am speaking of the emotional and spiritual cords that hold us together but cannot usually be seen. In fact, when we are connected, we may not fully realize it until the cord is broken. I would even go so far as to say that disconnection is the primary switch that turns out the light as the Darkness closes in.

Once the connection is broken, we define it in many ways until we "see" the cause. When we see the disconnection, we can begin to call it by name and take necessary steps to bridge the gap. All of this, as I have been saying, takes place in the dark.

The most profound revelation God gave me came during my second Christmas after divorce, when I had been divorced over a year. By this time, God had shown me many Lights toward the path out of Darkness, but there was more to come.

While waiting for a friend at a mall restaurant on Christmas Eve, I watched through the window as Christmas shoppers joyfully juggled packages in groups of three or more people, which I assumed were families. During my PDD, it seemed that everyone was happily married with their 2.5 children all settled under the roof of their happy little homes.

What was worse, all of these happy, happy families were at the mall doing last-minute shopping and enjoying the festive air and Christmas lights and music while I agonized over my solitude. My daughter was with her dad and I was sure they were enjoying a traditional Christmas—but they were not, as it turned out, because they were not a part of a real family either. Divorce had robbed all of us of the traditional family Christmas.

Later that evening as I lay in my friend's guest bedroom trying to go to sleep, I had a vision and a word from God. I saw a small child in the mall who had a helium balloon loosely tied to her wrist. Without warning the balloon came untied and began to float up to the high glass ceiling of the two-level mall. She gasped and cried out for someone to catch it. With that, her dad chased it, all the while reaching upward. Alas, he was not able to catch it, and the balloon floated to the high ceiling and stopped. It was too high for Dad to reach.

The message for me was that I felt like that balloon that had once been tied to someone's arm [my husband's] but was now floating away. The times when I felt loosed, I would cry out for someone, anyone to catch me.

Each time I felt disconnected, I cried out for help.

Each time someone allowed me to talk to her or him, I got connected.

Each time I went to the prayer closet and cried out to my Father to catch me, I got connected.

Each time I got ensconced in a book or writing project, I got connected.

Each time I heard a sermon on television or in church, I got connected.

Each time I took a "power, profession walk," I got connected.

Each time I attended a church meeting, I got connected.

If you miss everything I have written thus far, please do not miss this. If we get loose from someone precious or something (could be a job), remember to call for help to get reconnected.

The final word or parable: the Lord showed me that in my vision the balloon got away, but it was in the mall so it could not get out of sight or float away into oblivion. In this parable, the ceiling is a connection. When every other connection fails, our Father God is our ceiling. He will never let us float away without giving us a connection. He will never let us go.

There is Life out there. . . .

O f the many things I learned when walking out of Darkness was the fact that I could survive and that LIFE was waiting for me. The answer to the question about whether there is LIFE after divorce or depression, or in my case PDD [post-divorce depression], is a resounding YES and AMEN. What I endured made me not only stronger but gave me the freedom to do anything.

One young woman I knew years ago told me after the death of her mother at a relatively young age, "I always wondered whether I would be able to survive my mother's death when it was imminent, but I learned that if I survived losing my mother, I could survive anything." I echo her revelation.

There are things that each of us have hidden in our souls that we dread because they are inevitable. I never dreaded the kind of pain in divorce I would face because I did not see it coming. Nevertheless, I am a living testimony to the fact that you can not only come through but thrive after it is all over, no matter what "it" is.

I am not certain whether people ever overcome divorce as marriage is a soul tie; but I can say for sure that my life has been awesome the past sixteen years since the divorce. I have traveled and had experiences I would never have had if I was still married. Going through PDD made me more determined to be a Victor.

I give thanks to my Father God, His Son Jesus Christ, and the precious and every-present Holy Spirit who leads, teaches, and comforts through all of our trials. If you have made it this far in the book and do not know Jesus Christ in his power and presence, ask him now to become your Savior, your life, and your LIGHT out of Darkness. You will not regret this moment.

Whether you know Jesus Christ as Savior for many years or have just come to know him, I would love to hear from you about how this book affected you and ways that I might minister to others you know and love. Remember if you walk this road, be mindful of the ways in which you can show others the way out of Darkness.

Ministry has been the sole purpose of this work. I do lead workshops and help churches set up recovery groups and creative art ministries. Go and visit my website for contact information: www.dellbelew.com. Or write me at dbelew@dellbelew.com